THE MEDICI
OF FLORENCE

CONTENTS

5   Family Origins

20   Lorenzo and Giuliano

36   Misfortunes in Florence

48   Caterina, Queen of France

50   The Cadet Branch of the Family

51   Dukes and Grand Dukes: Cosimo I

66   Francesco I

78   Ferdinando I

81   Cosimo II

86   Ferdinando II

90   Cosimo III

Emma Micheletti

Family Portrait

THE MEDICI OF FLORENCE

Scala Books
Distributed by Lippincott & Crowell, Publishers

The myth of the Medici family's noble ancestry is not borne out by evidence; in fact the family can only be traced back to the end of the fourteenth century when they were living in the Tuscan Mugello, as they continued to do for some time. The Cafaggiolo branch of the family, farmers for generations, were the first to move to Florence, where they established themselves as merchants and bankers and quickly accumulated a fabulous fortune.

The founder of the family's wealth was Giovanni di Averardo (called Bicci) who lived from 1360 to 1429. He set about increasing his assets, which had already become sizeable towards the tail-end of the 1300's, by securing the contract for all municipal tax business. He had married Piccarda Bueri, born in Verona but of a Florentine family and known from then on by the affectionate nickname of 'Nannina.' The marriage produced four sons, two of whom did not survive infancy, and a daughter, who died on the eve of her wedding-day, about whom not even her name is known. On his death-bed, Giovanni said to his two remaining sons: 'I commend Nannina to your care: she has been a good wife to me and mother to you, and you must see to it that my dying does not deprive her of her rightful place in our family, nor of the honour and respect she has always deserved.' Cosimo and Lorenzo, hearing this charge, honoured and respected their mother, as well as heeding her advice to them, till the day she died.

Giovanni di Bicci was the instigator of that expansive artistic patronage for which all of the Medici with very few exceptions earned a lasting fame in Florentine life and history. He also set the trend for generous, liberal and easy hospitality which passed into a family tradition. It was Giovanni, for instance, who opened his doors to the anti-Pope John XXIII, the Neapolitan humanist Baldassarre Cossa, who died in 1419 while staying at the Medici house, and had the magnificent tomb built for him in the Baptistery in Florence on which Donatello and Michelozzo, two of the artists most favoured by the Medici, worked together.

Of Giovanni's two sons, the elder, Cosimo, was the head of the Cafaggiolo Medici's, the senior branch of the family, while Lorenzo was the founder of the Popolani line. During the period in which the Cafaggiolo's fortune was at a low ebb, members of the family being persecuted and sent into exile, it was the Popolani, the junior branch of the family, who evolved a political system based on democracy which gave rise to

Agnolo Bronzino (1503-1572):
Giovanni di Bicci
'At first glance he seemed severe and melancholic but those who knew him found his conversation pleasing and spirited.'

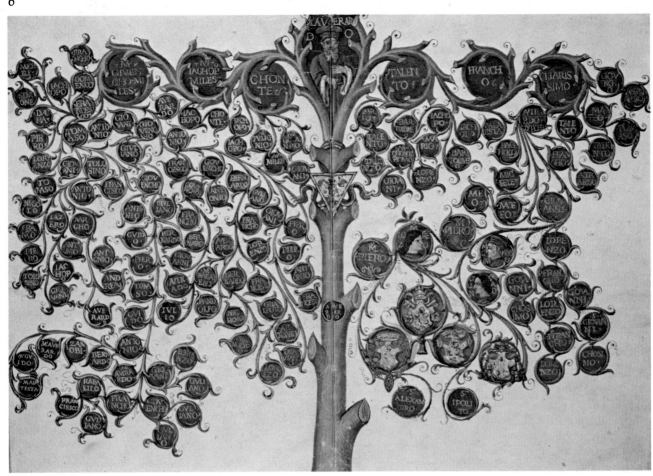

their reputation for having created a free republic of free citizens. Only later, when the principal line of the family had died out, did it fall to the Popolani to govern Tuscany which they did in ways which were anything but democratic.

Cosimo (1389-1464, known as 'the Elder' to distinguish him from the later Cosimo, the first Grand Duke), after inheriting from his father, began, as a private citizen, to play a leading role in the political and administrative life of the city, thus initiating the movement which was to bring the Medici to power without recourse to violence or actual conflict, unlike what happened with the Visconti and Sforza families in Milan, the Della Scala in Verona, the Este in Ferrara or the Mantuan Gonzaga family.

Cosimo's life was not an easy one, his position in Florence was always precarious because his enemies, the perennial Medici opponents, were plotting against him as early as 1431. Cosimo, having fallen foul of the Strozzi, the Pazzi, the Acciaioli and the Albizi families, was to suffer a period of solitary confinement in the tower of Palazzo Vecchio and only escaped death by poisoning after bribing his jailers. Then, in 1433, he was actually exiled; he went to Venice where the Venetians gave him a dazzling reception. But

he had only been there a year when the Florentines recalled him, feeling the need for his wisdom and diplomacy to guide the complex affairs of the Republic.

Cosimo did not leave the private *palazzo* in Via Larga which had been built by Michelozzo, but he gave the architect a further task, that of restoring the monastery of San Marco which he had bought in 1436 from the Salvestrini fathers and given to the Dominicans of Fiesole. He added the quiet cloisters and magnificent library, thereby creating one of the most harmoniously proportioned architectural complexes of the Florentine Renaissance. Cosimo then commissioned Fra Angelico to take on the work of decoration.

Cosimo did not give up the villas at Careggi, Cafaggiolo and Trebbio, and his successors followed suit, continuing his policy of holding the reins of power, and regulating the fortunes of the Florentine republic without ever setting foot inside Palazzo Vecchio or holding court in the true sense. The court that Cosimo presided over, like that of his immediate successors, was first and foremost a gathering of artists and men of letters from whose work and thought was created something of outstanding value, much prized by the Medici and the city of Florence alike: Dona-

Donatello and Michelozzo: Tomb of Anti-Pope John XXIII, Baldassare Cossa, commissioned by Cosimo the Elder.

Pontormo (1494-1556): Cosimo the Elder. Uffizi Gallery.

tello, Brunelleschi, Michelozzo, the Della Robbias, Filippo Lippi, Fra Angelico, Domenico Veneziano, Poliziano, Vespasiano da Bisticci, Platina and Pico della Mirandola were all, at some stage, employed by the Medici family. Cosimo was also a great bibliophile and by dint of generous financial outlay and indefatigable research he collected for his own library (it later became more or less public) incunabula, illuminated texts, manuscripts and parchments of immense value and artistic worth.

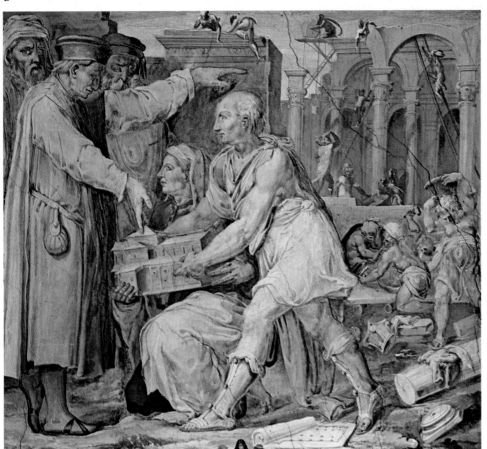

Vasari (1511-1574):
Brunelleschi presents Cosimo
the Elder with the project
for the church of San Lorenzo.
Palazzo Vecchio.

Illuminated manuscript
with page of music.
San Marco Library.

Illuminated manuscript, 15th
century: Palazzo Medici
during a performance of a
play about the Trojan War.
Cosimo the Elder said of this
palace, 'Too large a house for
such a small family'.

Vasari (1511-1574):
Cosimo the Elder returns
from exile. Palazzo Vecchio.
'...rarely was a citizen received
with such unanimous acclaim.'
(Machiavelli)

Fra Angelico (1400-1455):
Martyrdom of Saints Cosma
and Damian, patron saints of
the Medici. Cosimo the Elder
commissioned Fra Angelico the
frescoes and paintings in
San Marco.

The Library in San Marco,
commissioned by Cosimo the
Elder and built between 1436
and 1443, became the first
public library in Europe.

Donatello (1386-1466): Judith and Holofernes. This statue, now in Piazza della Signoria, was originally in Palazzo Medici.

Sandro Botticelli (1445-1510): Adoration of the Magi, detail of Cosimo the Elder. Uffizi Gallery.

Cosimo arranged that Florence should play host to the ecumenical Council which had been vainly working for years towards a reconciliation between the Roman Catholic and the Eastern Orthodox churches. The Pope, the Patriarch of Constantinople and the Emperor of Constantinople John VIII Paleologus were guests of the city of Florence and the Medici for the duration of the council, entertained with a spectacular display of pageantry, processions and banquets which seemed to transform the city into the centre of the universe.

Cosimo was at the same time a man of simple habits, and still felt a strong tie with the farming life he loved. He was also a good chess-player, a great reader of philisophical and moral works, and was always keen to make new contacts intellectually. Monarchs and popes alike counted him among their friends and he responded to their show of friendship (which so many would have given their eye-teeth for) with exceptional generosity and modesty. Perhaps it was precisely from the extreme simplicity of his way of life and working that the real charisma of the man drew substance; certainly he had no illusions that power and wealth could protect him from suffering in life and he bore its trials with equanimity, lived happily with his wife Contessina dei Bardi and greatly loved his sons Piero and Giovanni. He saw the latter as his presumptive heir, because Piero, the elder, had been afflicted since youth by a terrible arthritic condition, and it was not expected that he would live long. Giovanni, however, after living a life of pleasure frustrated his father's hopes for him dying in 1462 just over forty years old; his own only son had died only a few months before. This little boy of five had been named Cosimino after his grandfather and had won the old man's deep affection.

Cosimo died peacefully on 11 August 1464 in a state of spiritual tranquility; he remained lucid to the end, but he preferred to keep his eyes closed so that he might 'get used to the idea of never opening them again.' He was buried in the crypt of the Medici Basilica of San Lorenzo, where his massive tomb, resembling an enormous column which might almost have been built there

Mino da Fiesole (1429-1484):
Piero the Gouty.
National Museum (Bargello).

Benozzo Gozzoli (1420-1497):
Adoration of the Magi, fresco
in the chapel of Palazzo
Medici. (right) detail with
Cosimo the Elder and Piero
the Gouty (on the white
horse). (following pages) detail
with Lorenzo the Magnificent
as a young boy and his three
sisters Bianca, Maria and
Nannina.

as a buttress to sustain both Church and State, bore the words 'Pater Patriae' (Father of the Fatherland) after the name, given to him by the Republic of Florence.

His successor was Piero (1416-69), known as *Il Gottoso* (the Gouty), a shy, reserved man given to study, meditation, and the collection of beautiful objects. He had married Lucrezia Tornabuoni, who came from one of the noblest Florentine families and was a woman of profound spiritual perception, refined and cultured.

Piero for the five years in which he was in control, exerted his influence from behind the scenes in a completely informal way yet always rigorously observing the laws of the Republic; he proved to be a good politician and administrator and, like his father before him, drew on his own funds to help finance public welfare. He lived in the Palazzo in Via Larga, now Palazzo Medici Riccardi, though most of all he liked the Villa at Careggi.

But Piero too had his enemies, who endeavoured to wrest from him the real political initiative he held, on the pretext of liberating the city from imminent dictatorship. The conspirators (comprising those traditional Medici opponents, the Pitti, Acciaioli, Strozzi and Pazzi families) first made sure of outside support from the city of Ferrara, and then, on an assigned day, made an attempt to ambush his invalid's litter on its way down to Florence. But his son Lorenzo was out in front with an escort and used the successful tactic of drawing the assailants after him, thus alerting his father to change his route which he did. Piero reached Florence in safety and acted immediately to secure the support of the Milanese military divisions then stationed on the Tuscan border, with the result that he turned the tables on his attackers and, like his father before him, obtained the unconditional support of the Florentine Republic. Not even on that occasion did the Medici resort to acts of revenge or retaliation, but instead made a magnanimous peace proposal. By vociferous public acclaim Piero's leadership was endorsed for a further ten years. This was in 1466. But in 1469, only three years later, he was dead, leaving his son Lorenzo, later known as the Magnificent, as his successor.

Domenico Ghirlandaio (1449-1494): detail of Lucrezia Tornabuoni, wife of Piero the Gouty.
Santa Maria Novella.

Verrocchio (1435-1488): Tomb of Piero the Gouty and his brother Giovanni. San Lorenzo.

THE MEDICI COAT-OF-ARMS

In 1466 Louis XI, King of France, after meeting Piero the Gouty who was in France on a diplomatic mission, bestowed on him, as a gesture of friendship and admiration, the privilege of using the French fleur-de-lis on his coat-of-arms. The King's proclamation read: 'I, Louis, whom God has seen fit to make King of France, do hereby confer on Piero dei Medici and on his heirs and successors both born and yet to be conceived in legal matrimony, the right from this time hence and for evermore to have and to bear three fleur-de-lis upon their coat-of-arms.'

So it was that the arms of the House of Medici (red balls on a gold background) took on this new appearance. One of the balls, the one in the centre at the top, eventually was changed to blue with the motif of three fleur-de-lis embossed in

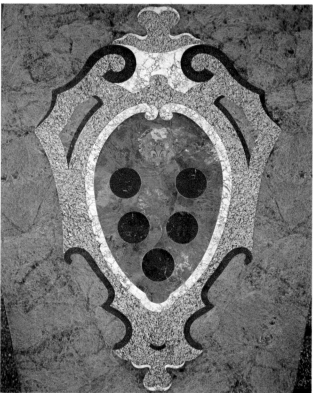

Medici coat-of-arms with French fleur-de-lis.

Medici coat-of-arms.

gold. Later Lorenzo reduced the total number of balls from seven to six. This is the coat-of-arms which, in various shapes and forms would become the symbol not only of the Medici but of the city itself.

Besides the family arms each individual member had his personal symbol. Cosimo the Elder had three plumes which can be seen on the caps of Lorenzo's three sisters in the famous Gozzoli fresco. Piero's heraldic device was a falcon holding in its beak a ring studded with cut diamonds, symbolizing strength and perseverance. Like his father, and later his son Lorenzo, he adopted the motto 'semper' (for ever).

THE FIRST MEDICI VILLAS

The villa at Trebbio was restored by Cosimo the Elder. Michelozzo was the architect who changed this villa from a severe medieval castle with a watch tower and enclosed courtyard into a luxurious country residence. At a later date Giovanni delle Bande Nere lived here and it was from here that his son Cosimo, after the assassination of Alessandro (1537), left for Florence to become first Grand Duke of Tuscany.

The villa at Cafaggiolo.

The villa at Careggi.

Cosimo the Elder commissioned Michelozzo to build the villa at Cafaggiolo in 1451. Originally the villa was enclosed by a wall with a moat and a drawbridge as can be seen in the lunette painted by Utens in 1599. The sons of Lorenzo the Magnificent lived in this villa with their mother, Clarice Orsini, and their tutor, Agnolo Poliziano. It was here that Pietro dei Medici, son of Cosimo I, murdered his young wife, another Eleonora of Toledo.

The villa at Trebbio.

Utens: Cafaggiolo, detail.

The courtyard of Cafaggiolo.

Careggi was another of the Medici villas rebuilt by Michelozzo for Cosimo the Elder. The crenellations visible under the roof give it an unmistakeable medieval appearance. Careggi was Piero the Gouty's favorite villa and became the seat of the Platonic Academy founded by the humanist Marsilio Ficino, tutor of Lorenzo the Magnificent.

When the Medici were sent into exile in 1494, the villa was looted and burned. The Grand Duke Cosimo I had it restored and decorated with frescoes by Pontormo and Bronzino; his successors, however, abandoned it and it fell once more into ruins. Today the villa is part of the hospital complex at Careggi.

Sculpture in the garden of Careggi.

LORENZO
AND GIULIANO

Lorenzo the Magnificent (1449-92) is undoubtedly the most interesting character as well as being the leading figure in the history of the Cafaggiolo branch of the Medici. Indeed he is one of the most significant figures in Italy of that era which saw the greatest blossoming of intellectual and artistic achievement in Florence especially.

Born in Florence in 1449 when the city was still nominally under republican rule, Lorenzo was the eldest son of the leading family in Florence and one that commanded considerable wealth. He lived an essentially private life, albeit a sumptuous one, while being groomed for the day he would inherit the burden of political power (the exact nature of which could not perhaps have been foreseen). Men of letters and philosophers gave him his instruction in those disciplines in which he would later prove proficient in his own right; as a poet, writer and thinker. The big fresco by Benozzo Gozzoli of the *Procession of the Magi*, painted in 1459 in the chapel of Palazzo Medici depicts some members of the Medici family at the time of the ecumenical

15th-century painted drum.

Florentine wedding chest of the 15th century.
Civic Museum, Tours

Piero di Cosimo (1461-1521):
Simonetta Vespucci.
Condé Museum, Chantilly.

SIMONETTA IANVENSIS VESPVCCIA

THE PAZZI CONSPIRACY

Bronzino: Giuliano dei Medici.

of the conspirators were arrested on the scene of the crime; those who escaped were pursued relentlessly as far as Turkey, as in the case of Bernardo Baroncelli who was subsequently hanged in the courtyard of the Bargello. The young Leonardo da Vinci made a famous drawing of Baroncelli's dangling corpse. Lorenzo's vendetta against the conspirators was terrible and the way the people of Florence reacted was no less violent: the main church of Florence had been desecrated and the young Giuliano, who was well-loved in the city, had lost his life. As a consequence the conspiracy achieved exactly the opposite effect to that which had been intended: in other words, it brought about a consolidation of the power of the Medici and virtually presented Lorenzo with absolute authority over the city.

The Pazzi Conspiracy, so-called because the plot was hatched by the family of that name, was led by Cardinal Riario, nephew and protegé of Pope Sixtus IV together with many other traditional enemies of the Medici. They decided to attack in the Florence Cathedral, choosing the moment of the elevation of the Host as the signal for the massacre. A more vile and sacrilegious act can hardly be imagined even if it was supposedly done in the name of freedom. Giuliano fell in a pool of blood, after being stabbed by Francesco dei Pazzi's dagger. Lorenzo, fending off his attackers with his sword, took cover with other members of his family in the sacristy, and resolved to avenge his brother's death with the utmost ruthlessness; the clemency shown by his grandfather and father on earlier occasions was out of the question. Most

Medal of Lorenzo.

Melozzo da Forlì: Sixtus IV.

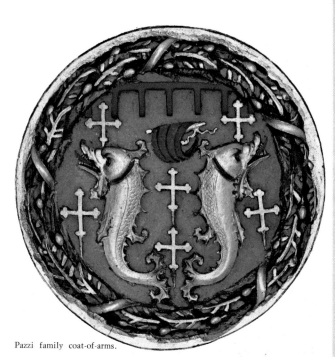

Pazzi family coat-of-arms.

Leonardo:
The hanging of Baroncelli.

Medal of Giuliano.

Verrocchio (1435-1488): Gentlewoman with a bunch of Primroses. National Museum (Bargello). This is probably a portrait of Lucrezia Donati, the great love of the young Lorenzo.

Council. Among the figures portrayed in it are Lorenzo and his brother Giuliano, still adolescents; the background is in every detail a court scene, recording a life style of a family which by that time was princely. The villa at Careggi was one of the places the family liked staying in most, along with the villa at Fiesole which commanded a panoramic view of Florence below.

The two brothers Lorenzo and Giuliano grew up together in a household which still retained some aspects of an upper middle-class life style. There are references in contemporary records to Giuliano's juvenile love affairs, which were idealized in the poetry and paintings of the time, notably by Agnolo Poliziano, Botticelli and Piero di Cosimo: in particular the beautiful Simonetta Vespucci Cattaneo, who died young and was most likely simply a platonic love of his, and Fioretta Gorini, by whom the young Giuliano had a son, Giulio, who later became Pope Clement VII, pontiff at the time of the Sack of Rome.

Lorenzo, at the age of twenty (in 1469), had married Clarice Orsini from Rome, the marriage having been arranged for the purpose of extending his family's connections to include the papal nobility. It was Lorenzo's mother Lucrezia Tornabuoni who had gone to Rome to meet her future daughter-in-law and had reported back to the bridegroom-to-be her impressions of the young woman: 'She isn't blonde, but then that isn't the custom here; I can't even tell if she has a nice bosom, she's so padded out with clothes.' Perhaps she was comparing her to her own daughters, Bianca, Lucrezia (called Nannina) and Maria who were much lovelier, more elegant and blonde after the fashion for women then in vogue in Florence, though the actual colour of their hair was no doubt achieved by long periods of sunbathing on the terrace of the house and perhaps owed something to expert treatment by the best hairdressers as well. Clarice, however, was very well-bred, considerate, perhaps a little submissive, and, in the simplicity of her own nature, intimidated by the culture and evident charm of

THE FINANCIAL EMPIRE OF THE MEDICI

The Medici fortune was based on the money accumulated by Giovanni di Bicci through his banking and tax collecting activities. Intelligent and prudent administration by his successors consolidated and augmented this fortune. Cosimo the Elder opened branches of the family bank in Flanders and in France and at one time even financed the King of England, Edward IV.

When Cosimo II closed the banks, the family itself went into decline. Up to that moment the banks had flourished: after they were closed the money to meet the spiralling expenses of the Grand Duchy was cut off.

Gold florin.

Tuscan bankers.

Early Florentine strong-box.

An early Tuscan bank.

Domenico Ghirlandaio (1449-1494): Confirmation of the Franciscan Rule.
Sassetti Chapel, Santa Trinita.
Detail at right with Lorenzo the Magnificent.

Bronzino (1503-1572): Portrait of Lorenzo. From the series of Medici portraits done for Cosimo I.

Vasari (1511-1574): Lorenzo the Magnificent. Palazzo Vecchio.
'He was olive skinned and had a face that, while not handsome, had such a dignity and nobility of expression as to inspire reverence: he had a strange nose, was short sighted and had no sense of smell.' (Niccolò Valori).

Unknown 15th-century sculptor: Bust of Lorenzo the Magnificent.
National Museum (Bargello).

Medal of Lorenzo.
National Museum (Bargello).

LAVRENTIVS MEDICES · PETRI FILIVS ·

her future mother-in-law, who was well pleased with her, and decided that Clarice would be a worthy bride for her son.

The ensuing spectacular wedding was held in Florence, rather in the tradition required for the heir to a throne — albeit the Medici were a very long way (or so, at least, it seemed) from being in a position to aspire to regal power. The celebration included jousting and tournaments in which the handsome Giuliano was the main contender, though Lorenzo also took part, his costume bright with priceless gems, the plumes in his helmet set with rubies, his horse's saddlecloth studded with pearls. There were banquets, balls, concerts in the open air, all at enormous expense which was met out of the Medici's private funds.

28

School of Vasari:
Lorenzo surrounded by artists
and poets.
Palazzo Vecchio.

Domenico Ghirlandaio (1449-
1494): Zachariah in the Temple.
Santa Maria Novella.
Detail with the portraits of
Marsilio Ficino, Cristoforo
Landino, Agnolo Polizano and
Gentile de' Becchi.

The numerous and impressive wedding presents included gifts from the Kings of France and Naples, the Dukes of Ferrara, Mantua and Milan.

Lorenzo himself was certainly not an attractive man to look at: he had a weak mouth, protruding eyes (he was also shortsighted) and an inordinately long nose. However he must have been a man of extraordinary personal charm, a quality he used to advantage in his political career as well as in his affairs of the heart. While still very young, he had fallen in love with Lucrezia Donati, who may have been the model for Verrocchio's *Gentlewoman with a bunch of Primroses* now at the Bargello, which seems to anticipate, in what the smile does and does not say, the later art of Leonardo da Vinci. Besides, Florence itself was a city of beautiful young women whose charms regularly bewitched the hearts of the two young Medici. What is more, Lorenzo's inclination towards the fair sex did not abate after his marriage; the truth was that, apart from his children and his obligations as a father, there were no strong ties between him and his wife, who was too different from him in her tastes, habits and upbringing; and when she died, still young, in 1487, he was not grief stricken. He was at that time deeply involved (to the intense displeasure of Francesco Guicciardini) with Bartolommea Benci Nasi, no longer a young woman but highly intelligent and most attractive to the forty-year old Lorenzo.

The two young Medici sons had also been brought up with a penchant for jousting and weap-

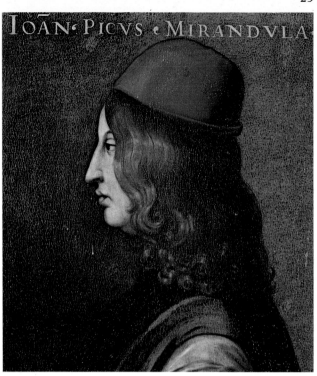

Anonymous:
Portrait of Pico della Mirandola.
Uffizi Gallery.

Ottavio Vannini (1585-1644):
Michelangelo presents his
sculpture of the Faun to
Lorenzo.

*Antonio del Pollaiolo (1431-
1448): Hercules and the Hydra.
Uffizi Gallery.*

*Andrea del Verrocchio (1435-
1488): Baptism of Christ.
Uffizi Gallery.
The work of Leonardo da Vinci,
then an apprentice in
Verrocchio's workshop, is
evident in the kneeling angel
on the left.*

ons, as was appropriate at that time for sons and heirs of powerful families. Lorenzo showed the extent to which he had benefited from that early instruction on 26 April 1478 when he courageously fought for his life and escaped assassination in the bloody attack unleashed inside the Cathedral of Florence by the Pazzi conspirators. The young Giuliano did not survive.

Lorenzo, by nature more inclined towards a cultivated mode of life rather than ostentatious living, was from the outset of his public career a great patron of the arts, following the tradition of his father and grandfather. He sponsored men of letters, artists and musicians, among them the organist and composer of religious music Antonio Squarcialupi was his particular favorite. But Lorenzo was also fond of dance ballads, serenades and popular songs of the time. Among his chosen

artists were Verrocchio, Pollaiolo, Ghirlandaio and Botticelli. It is perhaps significant that his first public appearance was on the occasion of the completion of Brunelleschi's dome when the great golden ball, surmounted by its cross, was set in position. There was in him the innate sensitivity of a writer and poet, qualities which had been fed by the cultural and artistic climate of Florence of this date. It may be that he even wished for a destiny other than that of a ruler and arbiter of power.

His, then, was a subtle intellect, well able to acquit itself in the highly problematical political arena of the times where the balance of power and aspiration was always on a knife-edge. Lorenzo knew how to reconcile the two, finding in the former, perhaps, the strength and resourcefulness to confront the latter with confidence.

In December 1479 he once again demonstrated his diplomatic skills in an attempt to restore peace to Italy and to resolve the conflict between the Duke of Milan and the King of Naples from which Tuscany, and Florence in particular, suffered, situated as it was between the two warring factions. He set out for Naples and gained an interview with King Ferrante of Aragon. Even then he did not refer to himself as the ruler of Florence, and in a letter written from Pisa to the Gonfalonier of the Republic, Pier Soderini, he explained that since the hostility of the house of Aragon was principally directed against him personally, the best thing he could do in the circumstances — in order to make sure of peace for Florence — was to deliver himself into their hands. The *Signoria*, or governing body of Florence, responded by granting him complete authority and freedom to negotiate.

The mission, which could have ended in disaster was, as it turned out, a success and a personal triumph for Lorenzo thanks to his political acumen and also, no doubt, due to the effect of his exceptional personal charm on King Ferrante. The King immediately withdrew from the anti-Florence coalition. In Spring 1480, on his return to Florence, Lorenzo carried with him a signed treaty which gave back to the city of Florence all the territories she had previously lost.

Lorenzo's third area of activity was that of financier and banker, following in the family tradition, although he did not have quite the right touch or flair for this sort of work. Such was his life-style that he did not particularly enjoy accruing wealth preferring to spend his fortune on helping artists, decorating his home, encouraging promising young sculptors, and building his splendid villas which were amongst the first in what was to become later a whole string of Medici country residences. In April 1492, a few months before the discovery of America, Lorenzo died in the villa at Careggi at the age of only forty four. Agnolo Poliziano and Pico della Mirandola were present at the end, and, according to an account by two of Lorenzo's most trusted aides, also there at his bedside was Girolamo Savonarola who prayed for him, for the redemption of Florence (which he had been branding as a pagan city) and then gave him benediction. This version of events is in contrast with that very much more dramatic account which has Savonarola relentlessly castigating the ruler of Florence: it would seem very unlikely that the famous friar, despite his fiery reputation, would have put aside his obligations as a priest and minister of God in the presence of a dying man.

Lorenzo the Magnificent's vases in the Museo degli Argenti in the Pitti Palace.

Agate vase with late 16th-century mounting.

Quartz cup with 15th-century mounting.

Vase in semi-precious stone with mounting by Giusto of Florence (c 1465).

Vase in semi-precious stone with late 15th-century French mounting.

THE 'PIAGNONI' AND THE 'ARRABBIATI'

Girolamo Savonarola, whom history traditionally casts as the greatest enemy Lorenzo dei Medici ever had, was born in Ferrara in 1452. He studied medicine and literature, but at the age of twenty, driven by his profound aversion for the corruption of the world, became a Dominican monk. He then began to preach his terrible sermons lashing out at the customs of the time and prophesying ruin and disaster for the city of Florence. The city was soon split into two opposing factions: the Arrabbiati (or angry protestors), who declared themselves for the Medici, and the Piagnoni (or miserable brigade), passionate supporters of the friar. When Savonarola's fury turned on Pope Alexander VI Borgia and the corrupt conduct of the Roman Curia, he was summarily banned from preaching. His

Savonarola.

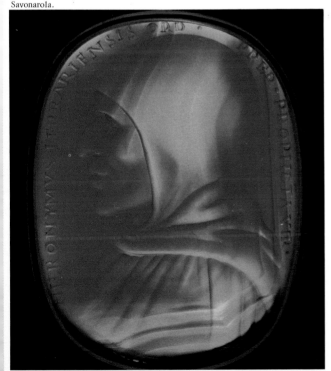

The death of Savonarola.

refusal to undergo a trial by fire (a common practice of the time) in order to prove that he was divinely inspired, aroused the antagonism of the Florentines who came to think of him as no more than a charlatan. Together with a few supporters he was allowed to live on in the monastery of San Marco where he had been Prior since 1491. But on 8 April 1498, the cells, cloisters and even the church of San Marco were invaded and desecrated during a ruthless hunt for the friar who voluntarily handed himself over to the Florentine Republic. On 23 May of the same year he and two of his followers were hanged, and after their bodies had been burned on the pyre, the ashes were thrown into the Arno. The execution took place in Piazza della Signoria, on a spot since marked by a commemorative stone.

Lorenzo's untimely death was unexpected. His son Piero and indeed the city itself had been lulled into a sense of security by his instinct for maintaining a political equilibrium and were not prepared to have to face the future suddenly without such a leader at the very moment when the French King Charles VIII was massing his troops for the invasion of Italy. Within a very short time the Medici had fled from Florence, which reverted to a Republican government.

Piero (1472-1503), Lorenzo dei Medici and Clarice Orsini's first born, was very different from his father and perhaps more like his mother, not least in his indifference to every form of culture and art. He did not, for instance, recognize the genius of Michelangelo who had grown up with him from childhood in his father's house, preferring to humiliate him by making Michelangelo build snowmen for his amusement, and rejecting the example of his father's political acumen for that of his Spanish footman, a champion sportsman in running and wrestling. Piero was, without doubt, politically inept.

Charles VIII invaded Italy with the intention of seizing the Kingdom of Naples; the latest installment in the longstanding struggle between France and Spain for domination of that territory. It is unlikely that he had designs on Tuscany, and Florence had two options: either they could have refused Charles' army transit through their territory, or otherwise granted him through passage while imposing conditions advantageous to themselves and maintaining a position of neutrality. But in 1494, Piero faced the French King's troops at the gates of the city, and probably overestimating the size and strength of the enemy forces, lost his head. He set out for the King's tents already a beaten man, indeed, he wrote to his secretary Bibbiena he felt himself to be already 'in the power of the King of France without hope of any favorable concession.' It is understandable that the French should have taken full advantage of his position, which they promptly did, demanding the fortress of Sarzana and the cities of Pisa, Livorno and Pietrasanta. All this was granted them and described by the French historian Philippe de Commynes: 'those who negotiated with Piero... were amazed at how freely and unhesitatingly he gave into them, so that everything was agreed without the least delay.' What this meant was that the young Medici himself had, almost from personal choice, opened the gates of Florence to Charles VIII — and when he came back into the city, he found the citizens united against him. He had no option but to make his

MISFORTUNES IN FLORENCE

Bronzino (1503-1572): Piero, son of Lorenzo the Magnificent, known as Piero the Unfortunate. He was responsible for the surrender of Florence to Charles VIII (1494).

Unknown Florentine (15th century): Charles VIII. National Museum (Bargello).

Francesco Granacci (1469-1543): Entry of Charles VIII into Florence. Uffizi Gallery.

Anonymous: Portrait of Cesare Borgia. Palazzo Venezia, Rome.

their assets before disguising herself as a nun and joining her husband in exile.

The Medici party wanted to regain the power they had so ineptly lost and Piero made several attempts to return as ruler of the city which had angrily driven him out, resorting to every means at his disposal and prepared to settle for any compromise he could get. In 1501, during his exile in Rome, he allied himself with Cesare Borgia, Duke Valentino, a man utterly devoid of scruples who was hungry for power and wealth. Borgia then conscripted troops from Louis XII of France, Charles VIII's successor with whom he had an alliance, and with this mercenary army marched to Barberino di Mugello, demanding that Florence open its doors to the fugitive Piero still regarded by the Florentines as a traitor. Cesare Borgia undoubtedly took this line of action not because he believed in Piero, but because he hoped the gratitude of the weak and cowardly Medici would ensure his own dominion over Central Italy.

The Republic of Florence did not yield to the pressure of his requests and promises: instead, it paid off Borgia in cash with golden florins, thus inducing him to pocket his profit and leave his unfortunate ally to his own fate. But still Piero would not give up: he joined his own meagre forces with those of the other Medici and the Orsini family, and attempted to mount an armed attack on the Republic. On this occasion Louis XII, at the invitation of the Gonfalonier Pier Capponi (who had previously been an ambassador in France), intervened to dissuade Piero to give up his futile enterprise. Whereupon the

escape, together with his brothers Giovanni (the future Pope Leo X who was dressed as a friar) and Giuliano, and his cousin Giulio, son of his uncle Giuliano. Florence had had enough of being ruled by young inexperienced men: Piero was only twenty two at the time. While the four Medici took refuge in Bologna, Piero's young bride Alfonsina Orsini stayed on in Florence for another year in order to salvage what she could of

Raphael (1483-1520):
Pope Leo X.
Uffizi Gallery.

latter resigned himself both to the fact that he would never succeed and to the inevitability of permanent exile from Florence. He died in 1503 from drowning in the Garigliano river in southern Italy.

Having suffered a setback in Florence, the Medici family fortunes found new life in Rome in the person of Giovanni, Lorenzo's second son, who had been sent away as a very young boy in order to be prepared for the church. Actual vocation, as was almost commonplace in those days, had nothing to do with the decision; it was rather a matter of political expediency and, in Giovanni's case, the intransigent will of the great man he had for a father. Born in 1476, the young Giovanni received the tonsure when he was little more than seven years old. From then on, as a mark of respect, all his relatives, including his father, called him 'Messer Giovanni' and ad-

dressed him in the formal way ('voi' instead of 'tu'). He was appointed Apostolic Protonotary by Pope Innocent VIII. At the age of thirteen he was made a Cardinal, in secret because of his age. When he reached sixteen, he became a *de facto* Cardinal with all the privileges and honours accruing to that office. Before the Council of Trent (1545-1563) the position of Cardinal was often given to the second-born sons of noble and influential families. Giovanni took holy orders only after his election to the papacy, which took place on 11 March 1513. He became a priest on 15 March and a bishop on the 19th. Thus, ten years after the death of Piero and nineteen since the family had been forced to leave Florence, the name of the Medici regained its aura of magnifi-

MACHIAVELLI AND THE MEDICI

Niccolò Machiavelli (1469-1527) was a member of the republican government of Florence that was set up after the expulsion of Piero dei Medici in 1494. When the Medici returned to power under Giuliano, Duke of Nemours (1512), Machiavelli was at first considered an enemy. He was accused of complicity in the plot of Piero Paolo Boscoli and Agostino Capponi against the Medici and imprisoned. From his prison he wrote two sonnets to Giuliano and, perhaps because of them, he was freed.

Lorenzo, Duke of Urbino.

Machiavelli.

In the same year he wrote The Prince *which he dedicated (1516) to Lorenzo, Duke of Urbino, son of Piero the Unfortunate and grandson of Lorenzo the Magnificent. Lorenzo had conquered the Duchy of Urbino with the help of Prospero Colonna having been too cowardly to accept Francesco Maria della Rovere's challenge to single combat in order to avoid war. Lorenzo had begun to show himself worthy of Machiavelli's dedication: 'A prudent ruler can not (nor should he) keep his word when doing so is contrary to his interests.'*
To another Medici, Pope Clement VII, Machiavelli dedicated his Florentine History, *which consisted of eight books containing the history of the city from the fall of the Roman Empire until the death of Lorenzo the Magnificent.*

cence, this time in the most prestigious state in the civilised world.

From his father the new pope had inherited taste and the generosity of a great patron. Perhaps these are the qualities for which he is best remembered for his pontificate, lasting nine years, was not only marred by the indiscriminate sale of indulgences to raise money for the papal coffers, but also saw the emergence of Martin Luther and the revolt of the Northern European Protestants against the Roman church.

From 1515 Michelangelo was working on plans to build a spectacular façade for the basilica of San Lorenzo, the Medici family church; he presented the designs to the new pope, but Leo X had more pressing concerns to attend to, and in fact the project was never begun.

It was several years before Michelangelo, commissioned by Clement VII, was able to work on the building of the burial chapel for Lorenzo Duke of Urbino and Giuliano Duke of Nemours generally known as the New Sacristy of San Lorenzo, to distinguish it from the Old Sacristy which was designed by Brunelleschi.

It may be that Michelangelo's work was too austere for Leo, whose favorite artists included Raphael, who was very much a courtier in the papal entourage, Andrea del Sarto, Baccio Bandinelli, Donato Bramante and Baldassarre Peruzzi. He also patronized men of letters such as Bibbiena, Sadoleto and Pietro Bembo. There is no doubt that Leo X was conscious of the urgency for church reform, especially the need to impose on the clergy a more rigorous code of discipline as well as putting an end to the scandalous practice of the sale of indulgences; but there is no doubt that he did not act with sufficient single-mindedness of purpose to effect these reforms. And so he paid a high price for his lack of resolution in carrying out the measures recommended by the Fifth Lateran Council opened by Julius II in 1511 and closed in March 1517, for in that same year Martin Luther's revolt broke out.

Martin Luther was an Augustinian monk from Saxony, restless in spirit and possessing exceptional intelligence, whose fearless crusade against the Roman Church and the pope in particular increased in violence as the years went on. The pope's response was to excommunicate him which he did on 15 June 1520. Luther publicly tore up the document of excommunication before a crowd of his followers, thereby refusing to acknowledge the authority of the pope and creating the great schism within the church. From that moment on, the conflict between Luther and the Papacy was irrevocable.

Leo X died suddenly, at the age of 46. There has been much controversy over the cause of his death which, for some people, appeared to be unnatural. It could have been the result of the pope's excessive delight on hearing of the French defeat in Lombardy which brought on a seizure, or it might have been caused by poisoning. Probably both are wrong, the latter deriving from the nineteenth-century view of the Renaissance as the age of poison.

Vasari (1511-1574):
Leo X returns to Florence.
Palazzo Vecchio.

Bronzino (1503-1572):
Giuliano, Duke of Nemours.

Titian (1488-1576):
Cardinal Ippolito dei Medici.
Pitti Palace.

However, Leo X's term as pope had revived the fortunes of his family. It was his brother Giuliano, who had inherited most of the charisma and intelligence of his father Lorenzo, who was the first to return to Florence in 1512, after an exile which had lasted eighteen years. Giuliano was the youngest of Lorenzo and Clarice's children, born in March 1479 and was made much of by his parents and his grandmother. He was of a gentle disposition, but melancholic and introverted. He was popular with the Florentines during the months in which he governed the city on behalf of his brother Giovanni, then still a cardinal. He was by nature generous and conciliatory, a man not given to rancour or revenge, and he shouldered this manifestly difficult responsibility with notable success, winning the affection of many and the respect of even his enemies in the process. His democratic tolerance, which would clearly have been effective in furthering the Medici cause, did not appeal to his brother (who had in the meantime become pope) and still less to his cousin Giulio, later Clement VII, the most determined campaigner for the restitution of the family's rights in the city of Florence. So Giuliano was recalled to Rome, on the pretext of having been appointed Gonfalonier of the papal army. After only eight months rule he died and was succeeded by his nephew Lorenzo, Piero's son. In his dying words Giuliano had implored Lorenzo to hold to a love of peace and a keen sense of justice. Lorenzo, however, did not follow this advice and his rash political decisions made him an unpopular figure. Even the generally peaceful reinstatement of Giuliano met with some opposition, led by Pier Paolo Boscoli and Agostino Capponi, but their plot was badly organized, their aims uncertain and the conspirators gathered together in a somewhat haphazard way. The two ringleaders of the plot were beheaded in 1513.

Giuliano Duke of Nemours was without doubt one of the most humane figures in the whole Medici dynasty, and perhaps one of the most sensitive too. In an age when marriages were made for reasons of political and financial expediency, Giuliano's marriage to Philiberta of Savoy, was a love match. Philiberta was the sister of Duke Charles III of Savoy and Louise d'Angoulême, the courageous mother of Francis I of France. Their union was the cause of much gossip, especially on the subject of the bride's dowry on which Piero's widow Alfonsina Orsini waxed more eloquent than anyone. The house of Medici's attitude was that princesses of Savoy had always come to their husbands bearing considerable marriage dowries, yet in Philiberta's case it was the pope who had to provide his brother's wife with hers. In fact at that particular time the house of Savoy was in desperate straits and Philiberta's only financial security depended on the paltry feudal dividends from the regions of Fossano and Gex in Savoy.

So the wedding took place in Turin on 10 February 1515. The bride was '… tall, pale, very thin, hunchbacked and with a long nose.' She

Michelangelo (1475-1564):
Tomb of Giuliano, Duke of
Nemours.
New Sacristy, San Lorenzo.

was clearly no beauty, to go by this ruthless account of her by the Venetian ambassador Piero Pasqualigo. However, it should be said that her alleged hunchback appearance was more likely a roundshouldered posture often found in very tall people, and in fact Pasqualigo himself does go on to say: '...in any case, a fine looking woman.' Others refer to her as 'not beautiful, but a welcome presence.' Giuliano on the other hand was seen as 'the handsomest young knight of all.' The marriage was short lived. The young Duke fell ill that summer with pulmonary tuberculosis and died on 16 March 1516 when he was only thirty seven. His wife nursed him devotedly in this last illness; after his death she returned to France and died at Virieu at the age of twenty seven. All Florence mourned Giuliano's death: he was buried in the Basilica of San Lorenzo and subsequently commemorated by the stupendous tomb by Michelangelo in the New Sacristy.

Lorenzo, Duke of Urbino (1492-1519) was very different in character from Giuliano of Nemours. He was fiercely ambitious, and in this was encouraged, even goaded on by his mother Alfonsina Orsini's own immense ambition for him. The young Medici lost no time in casting covetous eyes towards the Duchy of Urbino where, as a child, during his exile, he had been both generously and lovingly looked after by the della Rovere family. Gratitude, however, like courage, was not one of Lorenzo's outstanding virtues. First of all he suffered a defeat at the head of an army of soldiers he had asked his uncle the pope to send him. Then came a noble offer from Francesco Maria della Rovere to resolve the issue with as little bloodshed as possible by a duel between the two of them with Urbino as the prize for the winner: Lorenzo refused and with a fresh army commanded by Prospero Colonna (and certainly through no merit of his own) he conquered the Duchy and usurped the Dukedom.

Through the pope's influence it was arranged

that he would marry Madeleine de la Tour d'Auvergne, a relative of the Bourbon family, seventeen years old, 'beautiful, and possessing many virtues and good qualities.' They were married in May 1518 in Paris. Lorenzo's excessive pomposity was not popular with the French; whereas the gentle youthfulness of Madeleine, who learned to dress in the latest Florentine fashion as soon as she arrived in the city, won her the enthusiastic admiration of the people, considerably more so than her husband who only made them regret that the humanely intelligent spirit of Giuliano was no longer with them.

Lorenzo's marriage was brief. He too soon contracted tuberculosis, the condition being made worse no doubt by his intemperate life style. They had a child, Caterina, destined for greatness in later life; but a few days after the birth the young mother died of puerperal fever and within a short time she was followed to the grave by her husband.

The second pope of the House of Medici was Clement VII; this was Giulio, son of Giuliano, the brother of Lorenzo the Magnificent, who had been assassinated in the Pazzi Conspiracy. Giulio was brought up with his cousins by Lorenzo and Clarice Orsini. There is some doubt over the identity of his mother, she may have been Fioretta Gorini, though nothing much is known about her and Giuliano had several mistresses at the time. The child's godfather was Antonio da Sangallo, the famous architect, and he began life in his mother's house in Borgo Pinti. She was a 'donna libera' that is, an unmarried woman. The young Giulio was then officially acknowledged by the Medici, took their surname, and became a legitimate child of the family. As a boy he was sent away to train for a career in the church, and through the good offices of Lorenzo the Magnificent, who proved his affection for the child by continually making representations on his behalf, Giulio was appointed Prior of Capua when he was only ten years old. Giulio was always considered as an equal member of the family whose fortunes he followed with unfailing devotion. He became pope in 1523 after the death of Hadrian VI. While he was pope, Italy suffered some of the most appalling calamities of the century; the whole country becoming the arena for the war between Francis I of France and the Holy Roman Emperor Charles V over the domination of southern Italy. In Rome the Colonna family, sworn enemies of the pope, formed a political alliance with the French (who were at that stage losing) and forced Clement to take refuge in the

Michelangelo:
Lorenzo, Duke of Urbino.
New Sacristy, San Lorenzo.

Castel Sant'Angelo. He was only saved by Spanish envoys sent to free him. The action of the French and the Colonna had been intended as a warning to the pope but he did not accept it as such, protesting to Paris and to London. Imperial reinforcements continued to cross the frontier

Vasari (1511-1574):
Clement VII appoints his
Cardinals.
Palazzo Vecchio.

into Italy heading for Rome, including the dreaded Tyrolean Landsknecht mercenaries led by Georg von Frundsberg. They were fervent Lutherans and were determined to humiliate the pope and the 'corrupt' cardinals of Rome. It was said that they carried with them a silken rope with which they intended to hang Clement. In fact the army marching on Rome was made up of a disorderly and starving mob which, having no real leadership, was happy to wreak havoc and pillage where ever it went. On 5 May 1527, after having laid waste to half of Italy, it encamped beneath the walls of the city of Rome. During the previous months of anxious waiting, Clement VII had appealed to everyone for aid, especially to the King of France, invoking their old alliance, but to no avail. He was alone, with his city at the mercy of the imperial troops. On 6 May, the walls were breached and the soldiers began to pour into Rome, rapidly spreading through the city determined to loot, destroy and murder. Once again the pope and his court took refuge in the Castel Sant'Angelo. The city remained at the mercy of this plundering horde whose acts of cruelty equalled those of the original barbarian invaders in the days of the Fall of the Empire. One month later Clement VII gave himself up and was compelled to accept the victors' harsh terms which included the payment of large sums of money, surrendering some of the territories of the papal states, and the taking of five prelates and three of the pope's relations as hostages. These were appalling impositions which the pope of necessity

Papal Bull of Clement VII.
Vatican, Secret Archives.

SCHISM AND REFORM: LUTHER AND HENRY VIII

The sale of indulgences was still a flourishing business during the papacy of Leo X. He was reported to have said, 'It has served us well, this myth of Christ.'
In 1517 Martin Luther's revolt against the church broke out. Luther was an Augustinian monk from Saxony whose pleas for reform in the church grew ever more insistent. The Pope's answer was to excommunicate him on 15 June 1520. Before a large group of his followers Luther publicly tore up the document; this denial of papal authority led inevitably to the great schism.

Holbein: Henry VIII.

Cranach: Martin Luther.

Clement VII, the second Medici pope, found himself in the midst of another serious schism. Henry VIII petitioned the pope to have his marriage to Catherine of Aragon annulled so that he might marry Anne Boleyn. Lengthy negotiations followed this request but neither side yielded and finally Henry repudiated Catherine, married Anne and had her crowned Queen in 1534. At this point there was still hope of avoiding the schism due to the intervention of the King of France; but even this came to nothing due to the intransigent opposition of Henry VIII. Henry was actually excommunicated by Clement's successor as Clement died in 1534.

Vasari (1511-1574):
Alessandro dei Medici.
Uffizi Gallery.

was bound to accept, imprisoned as he was in Castel Sant'Angelo. Finally, on 8 December, he succeeded in slipping through the guard and, disguised as a pedlar, accompanied by one faithful companion, he escaped to Orvieto, a frightened and haunted man. He was only 49, but already worn out by life. He lodged in appalling conditions in the Bishop's Palace which was by that time in ruins.

But the Sack of Rome was not the end of his troubles. Clement had barely emerged from his ordeal when he was confronted by another serious issue: the English Schism. King Henry VIII, wishing to marry the young Anne Boleyn, asked the pope to annul his marriage to Catherine of Aragon. There followed a protracted series of negotiations in which both sides used sophisticated dialectical argument without reaching any pos-

itive agreement. Finally Henry VIII refused to submit to the ruling of the pope and the Church of Rome and, in 1533, having divorced Catherine, married Anne who was crowned Queen in 1534. At that point there was still some hope, thanks to the intervention of the King of France, of avoiding the schism: but even this evaporated in the face of the intransigent opposition from Henry himself.

The final condemnation of the King of England came from Clement VII's successor (Clement died in 1534), with the excommunication of the monarch which in turn led to the birth of the new State religion with the King of England at its head.

If the papacy of Clement VII was tormented and tragic, it nonetheless kept the power of the Medici flourishing in Florence. With the death of Lorenzo Duke of Urbino in 1519, a new Medici appeared on the scene, Alessandro, whose existence up to that moment no-one seems to have been aware of. Perhaps he was an illegitimate son of the dead Duke, who had been a man much given to love affairs. Perhaps — and historians tend to give more weight to this interpretation — he was the son of the pope, born during the time when Clement was a cardinal. It was said that his mother was a negress or mulatto, a supposition borne out by the somewhat negroid features of the young Alessandro which gave him his nickname the Moor. It is probable that his mother was an ordinary peasant woman from the area around Rieti named Simonetta, who was in the service of Alfonsina Orsini Medici during the long period that she lived in Rome. Subsequently she married and, finding herself in abject poverty, she wrote a pathetic letter to Alessandro, signing herself 'your dear mother Simonetta.' But the young ruler of Florence, perhaps ashamed of his origins, did not lift a finger to help her.

This Alessandro, of obscure parentage, one of the most vicious members the Medici family ever produced, was in power at a time when Florence was under siege from the imperial troops, in that year of 1529 which saw the last determined stand of Republican resistance against Medici control. Michelangelo was fighting on the Republican side. After being so highly favored by Lorenzo the Magnificent only to be looked down on by Lorenzo's sons, Piero and Pope Leo X, Michelangelo had found a patron in the person of Clement VII who overlooked his Republican leanings and was keen that 'we should especially embrace Michelangelo to encourage him with as much kindness and peace of mind as possible so as to make him continue in conscientiousness and diligence with his work on the statues,' a reference to the famous statues for the Medici tombs in San Lorenzo. Clement was a great patron, in fact, a true Medici, and gave protection to Michelangelo, Baldassarre Castiglione, Niccolò Machiavelli (who dedicated the *Florentine Histories* to him), Giulio Romano and Sebastiano del Piombo.

After the imperial army's siege of Florence had been lifted (1529), Alessandro dei Medici was confirmed as the ruler of Florence in a pact between Clement VII (ever a zealous guardian of Medici power) and the Emperor Charles V when they met in Bologna.

However, the fine promises of 'the preservation of liberty' were never kept. Also at Bologna it was resolved by the Emperor and the pope that Alessandro should marry Charles V's illegitimate daughter Margherita. Evidently the Medici were aiming to forge yet more prestigious links for their family. But Alessandro was already unpopular and played for time before making his reappearance in the city as its ruler. Meanwhile the real controller of Florence was Baccio Valori, Clement VII's delegate, who paved the way for Alessandro's reinstatement as head of the Republic. Finally, in 1532, Alessandro became dictator of the city and Florence endured four and a half years of tyranny in the hands of a man whose unpopularity increased until his death in 1537. It was actually another Medici, Lorenzino, belonging to the cadet branch of the family, who brought about Alessandro's death in January 1537.

Lorenzino, a companion of Alessandro's in his dissolute way of life, managed to lure him into a trap by some sordid intrigue and stabbed him to death; possibly under the illusion that he would be able to seize power, and in his imagination, equating himself to the republican Brutus, the noble murderer of Caesar. Michelangelo's magnificent marble bust, now in the Bargello, can be interpreted in this light.

So the city was freed of its tyrant Alessandro, although in order to prevent outbreaks of insurrection and disorder there was no public announcement of his death. His body was taken by night to the church of San Giovannino, which was the nearest to Palazzo Medici, and the following night it was buried in the tomb of Lorenzo Duke of Urbino, who was thought at the time to have been Alessandro's father.

Two young members of the Medici family, contemporaries of Alessandro, were living in Florence at this time: Ippolito (1511-1535), the ille-

Michelangelo (1475-1564): Brutus, detail. National Museum (Bargello). It seems likely that in this portrayal of Caesar's assassin, Michelangelo wanted to pay homage to Lorenzino, who murdered the hated tyrant Alessandro.

gitimate son of Giuliano Duke of Nemours, and Caterina (1519-1589), born of the marriage of Lorenzo Duke of Urbino to Madeleine de la Tour d'Auvergne, great-grand-child of Lorenzo the Magnificent and last surviving heir of the senior branch of the Medici family. In Florence she was known as the 'Little Duchess' and lived in the Palazzo Medici with the gentle Ippolito to whom she was probably sentimentally attached. Also living in the Palace was Duke Alessandro. There is no doubt that Ippolito would have been a more suitable heir to the Medici fortune and power after the family's return from exile, and more acceptable to the Florentines by virtue of his generous and mild disposition inherited from his father. Clement VII, however, had championed Alessandro's cause and forced Ippolito, very much against his will, to take up a career in the church.

At the time of the Sack of Rome and the expulsion of the Medici from Florence, Caterina was only eight. However she did not go into exile with Ippolito and Alessandro, but, on the specific intervention of Clarice Medici-Strozzi, was commended to the new government of the Republic which in turn entrusted her to the *Murate*, a closed order of nuns living in a convent which the novices entered through a gap in the wall, that gap being bricked up again when they had passed inside. Hence the name *Murate*, meaning literally 'walled-in women' in Italian. It was the most celebrated convent in the city, the place where the daughters of high Florentine society were educated and therefore a fitting destination (all to fitting, perhaps) for Caterina, coming as she did from the hated Medici family by then exiled from Florence. Caterina stayed there until she was eleven, living from one day to the next possibly unaware of the mortal danger in which she lived due to her isolation. The threat to her life became serious during the siege of Florence (1529). Perhaps the government of the Republic had it in mind to hand her over as a hostage to the imperial victors, or perhaps they planned to take their revenge on her, the last representative of the senior branch of the Medici, for the ignominious defeat they had suffered, in part due to Medici treachery. These rumours reached the ears of the young Caterina who displayed exceptional strength of character and will. She cut off her hair, dressed herself as a nun and appeared before the officers of the Republic demanding to know if they would ever dare lay their hands on a sister of the Florentine convent: 'I will be seen in public dressed like this, so that the people can see who I am; a nun taken by force from her convent.' The fact that a nun from a cloistered order should be forced out into the world would have created a tremendous outcry against those responsible since the people of Florence had already been tried beyond endurance by the tribulations of the siege.

So it was that Caterina won her first battle. As a result she was transferred to the more obscure convent of Santa Lucia in the Via San Gallo, and there she awaited the return of her family from exile. Her subsequent marriage to Henry, the second son of Francis I, King of France, was negotiated by Pope Clement VII with that monarch in 1532. The match did not please the French. A descendant of bankers and merchants, a 'tradeswoman' in other words, was not worthy of the son of their king, even if Henry was not the Dauphin. However, Caterina was the daughter of

CATERINA, QUEEN OF FRANCE

a Duke, for all that the Duchy of Urbino had been only a temporary acquisition of her father Lorenzo's and had since been returned to its legitimate owners. In addition she was closely related to the pope. And so the marriage was accepted by the French people and the court as a *fait accompli*; the wedding was solemnised by the pope himself in Marseille on 28 October 1533.

Caterina's destiny was in the meantime about to lead her life onto a very different course. The sudden early death of the Dauphin meant that her husband came to the throne as Henry II, and after his death she assumed power as a firm and dependable Queen Regent, in place of her children, born after ten years of sterility and who were either under age or unfit to rule at the death of their father. From that moment, however, Caterina's life is no longer an integral part of Medici history; but rather belongs to the history of the Valois and the French royal family.

François Clouet (1510-1572): Henry II of France and Caterina dei Medici, surrounded by members of the French royal family.

Vasari (1511-1574):
The wedding of Caterina and
Henry II.
Palazzo Vecchio.

Caterina receives the Polish
ambassador. Detail of a
tapestry.
Uffizi Gallery.

With the marriage of Caterina, the senior branch of the Medici family came to an end. Now in the changing fortunes of the family and their struggle for power over Florence there came to the fore the cadet branch of the Medici, descended from Lorenzo, the brother of Cosimo the Elder, who was nicknamed 'Popolano' because of his undisguised sympathy for democracy. The most outstanding of these Popolani was the son of Giovanni delle Bande Nere and Maria Salviati, Cosimo, who was at this time preparing to assume control of the city.

Cosimo was the first true Duke of Florence, later created Grand Duke, and it was he who laid the foundations of the Medicean principality which was to continue without interruption for the next two centuries.

Giovanni delle Bande Nere (1498-1526), who gave the name of *bande nere*, or black squads, to his companies of soldiers as a sign of mourning for the death of Leo X, was the son of Caterina Sforza and Giovanni il Popolano. He was first and foremost a man at arms, a *condottiero* of great courage, to whom some historians have attributed the reawakening of patriotic feeling among Tuscans, whereas in fact he was simply a soldier of fortune whose allegiance wavered between the French and the Spanish in accordance with the

THE CADET BRANCH OF THE FAMILY

Bronzino (1503-1572):
Pierfrancesco the Elder.

Bronzino (1503-1572):
Giovanni il Popolano.

Bronzino (1503-1572):
Giovanni delle Bande Nere.

prevailing current. Nonetheless he was an able and valiant leader of men and died with stoical heroism at the age of twenty-eight, at Governolo near Mantua, of a gunshot wound inflicted by Alfonso I d'Este. His wife was Maria Salviati, who was also related to the Medici. Maria was an austere figure, but sensitive, intelligent and cultured. It was perhaps not a felicitous match, but the future Cosimo I's personality was a combination of the positive and negative aspects of his father's character (though he did not inherit his courage) and the intelligence, prudence and intellectual relish for art of his mother. Maria Salviati was widowed while still very young, after which she withdrew to the Castello del Trebbio in the Mugello: there, more out of economic necessity than a love of solitude, she brought up Cosimo, keeping him out of the way of the changing fortunes of the Medici following the Sack of Rome and the Siege of Florence, and waited for more auspicious times when Cosimo could make a bid for power.

That day came suddenly, the morning after the murder of the hated Alessandro in 1537. The four counsellors of the Florentine Republic, Filippo Strozzi, Niccolò Accaioli, Baccio Valori and Francesco Guicciardini, offered the Dukedom to the eighteen year old Cosimo. Perhaps they thought that they were dealing with a young man whom they could manipulate as they pleased, but in this they were mistaken. Cosimo was determined to take absolute control immediately and proceeded to free himself from his councillors.

Filippo Strozzi and Baccio Valori were among those who subsequently left Florence to go into exile in Venice. Francesco Guicciardini retired in a fury to his villa in the hills above the city. Maria Salviati did not approve of her son's action, and took especial pains to remind him of the magnanimity of Filippo Strozzi to whom she had appealed in those difficult early years and who had given her most generous assistance. She wrote in these terms to her son. But in return, she received neither solicitude nor affection, only indifference, even if it is not true that Cosimo never saw his mother again after being created Duke of Florence. While she was living alone, for the most part at Trebbio or in other Medici villas, Maria wrote letters which prove how closely she kept in touch with her son's life and with her daughter-in-law as well as showing her tender concern for her many grandchildren.

The exiles did not give up the struggle. In the same year of 1537, they mustered an army commanded by Piero Strozzi, Filippo's son, which,

DUKES AND GRAND DUKES: COSIMO I

Semi-precious stone inlays of the coats-of-arms of some of the cities which formed the Grand Duchy of Tuscany. Chapel of the Princes, San Lorenzo.

with the support of the French met the Florentine forces reinforced by imperial troops and led by Alessandro Vitelli. (Unlike his father, Cosimo had no great liking for weapons or for fighting battles). The battle took place at Montemurlo near Prato on 31 July and was won by the joint Florentine-imperial forces. Filippo Strozzi and Baccio Valori were among those taken prisoner. Strozzi ironically was beheaded in the Fortezza di San Giovanni (known as the Fortezza da Basso) to which he had made such generous financial contributions. Cosimo, however, was not given to gratitude or mercy and confiscated all his wordly goods.

In the years that followed, Cosimo's dominion was steadily extended to cover the whole of Tuscany, until in April 1555, after a ruthless siege,

he subdued his most implacable enemy, the Republic of Siena. And when in 1559 Montalcino also ʃurrendered to him, his campaign was complete and Tuscany had become a single unified state.

His military conquests over, Cosimo proved his true greatness in his peacetime achievements. At his instigation work was begun on the construction of the port of Livorno (Leghorn); methods of agriculture were improved by the use of the most modern equipment then available; the country areas were repopulated, and even in the Maremma region redevelopment projects were attempted. The cities of Tuscany were enriched with new works of art and architecture, especially Florence, the capital city. The Duchy became a Grand Duchy in 1569 following imperial intervention.

This Duchy, with its absolute despotic control over the city and the region, was created through the efforts of Cosimo a descendant of those Medici who, during the exile first of Piero and later of Alessandro and Ippolito, had sided with the Republic and come out openly in support of it, and had even changed their name to Popolano by way of demonstrating their democratic sentiments. Cosimo was anything but a democrat and demonstrated this most clearly by transferring his 'court' from the Palazzo Medici in via Larga to Palazzo Vecchio, which had been since earliest mediaeval times the centre of civic power. In 1539 he married Eleonora, the daughter of the Viceroy of Naples, Don Pedro of Toledo. Eleonora was beautiful, in fact the most beautiful and enchanting bride ever to cross the Medici threshold; fair with blue eyes, a perfectly oval-shaped face, and of noble bearing. Her husband was much in love with her, so that this turned out to be no *mariage de convenance* (even if it had started as such) but a love match. Eleonora however was not popular with the Florentine people. They felt she was remote, and possibly imagined that she was proud because of her near-royal lineage. Florentines were used to the straightforward (albeit cultured and intellectual) familiarity which had typified earlier women of the household. Eleonora was not given to walking on foot through the streets of the city, nor riding on horseback; instead, she insisted on travelling in her sedan-chair, which was upholstered in velvet and green silk, almost invariably with the curtains lowered. But perhaps her beauty and the charm that emanated from her — dressed as she was in sumptuous clothes of the most exquisite kind, and adorned with magnificent jewels for which she had a particular predilection —

Vasari (1511-1574):
Cosimo I studies battle plans
for the conquest of Siena.
Palazzo Vecchio.

Anonymous (1561):
Entrance of Duke Cosimo I
into Siena.
State archives, Siena.

Vasari (1511-1574):
The project for enlarging
Florence. Palazzo Vecchio.

helped her to win their hearts. She was an intelligent woman from a wealthy family, possibly even richer than her husband, and a first-rate administrator of her own and Cosimo's shared assets. She it was who bought the large *palazzo* on the hill south of the Arno (the original design of which was by Brunelleschi) from the Pitti family whose overreaching ambition had ruined them.

She was benevolent by nature, providing largesse from her personal funds for the poor children of the city. Compassionate and deeply religious in the traditional Spanish way, she was not bigoted even if she did persuade her husband to allow the Jesuits (who had previously been ex-

pelled from the city) back into Florence. Adored by her husband, who had chosen as her heraldic emblem a lapwing hatching out her young, she returned his love in equal measure and if ever she was unable to accompany him on his travels would write him long letters full of affection and tender advice.

Initially Cosimo had ordered a large suite of rooms in Palazzo Vecchio for her, designed by Giorgio Vasari and frescoed by Bronzino, these two having been appointed Court architect and painter. Then, after the move to Palazzo Pitti, it was for Eleonora and her growing family (the grand-ducal couple had eleven children) that Cosimo put in hand the landscaping of the great Boboli garden, commissioning Tribolo and Buontalenti to carry out the work. The beautiful Spaniard Eleonora, who was accustomed to the Neapolitan sunshine, had never been able to resign herself to the severity of the surroundings of Palazzo Vecchio, enclosed by stone walls and looking out onto the austere symmetry of the *piazza*. This was before the construction of the Uffizi, that magnificent wing facing the Arno which Vasari built on the Duke's orders between 1564 and 1574 after Eleonora's death. Cosimo was determined that Florence should be transformed through his building programmes into a capital

The Port of Leghorn, in semi-precious stones. Uffizi Gallery. Another great 'work of peace' of Cosimo's was the creation of the port of Leghorn.

Vasari: Apotheosis of Cosimo I. Palazzo Vecchio. Such was the Grand Duke's glory that Vasari thought nothing of portraying him as a deity.

Vasari:
Portrait of Cosimo I.
Palazzo Vecchio.

Vasari:
Arrival of Eleonora of Toled‹
at the villa of Poggio a Caianc
Palazzo Vecchio.

city on a par with any in Europe.

Eleonora died when she was only forty. Already ill with tuberculosis, she was on a journey to Pisa when she and two of her children fell ill with malignant fever. The two youngsters died a few days before she did; Giovanni's death caused her the most appalling suffering, while that of Garzia was concealed from her for the last two days of her life. She died on 17 December 1562.

Although we are concerned here with the history of the Medici family, it would be nonetheless inappropriate to say nothing of Vasari, Cosimo I's architect or of Benvenuto Cellini who offered his services to the Grand Dukes on returning from his adventures at the Sack of Rome and Fontainebleau. Vasari practically created the new city of Florence, improving on the layout between the Palazzo Vecchio, the Uffizi extension to the river and the loggia of the Signoria, perfectly blending the fourteenth-century buildings with the classicism of his own addition which had originally

Vasari:
Portrait of Eleonora of Toledo.
Palazzo Vecchio.

been intended to house public offices. Vasari then set to work on the raised passageway which linked the Uffizi (already connected to Palazzo Vecchio) to Palazzo Pitti; an aerial route which provided direct access for the Grand Duke between his Palace and the state offices, later to be called the Vasari Corridor. This structure is supported by arches on the Lungarno, then crosses over Ponte Vecchio, and passes through houses in Via Guicciardini; at one point it is reduced to a narrow gallery which skirts the tower of the Mannelli family who would not allow the corridor to pass through their property. In response to this blank refusal, the Grand Duke instructed Vasari to find a solution by taking the structure around the outside of the Mannelli premises since 'every one of us,' as he put it, 'is master in his own house.'

Michelangelo never worked for Cosimo, being by that time an old man and settled in Rome, but Benvenuto Cellini completed the *Perseus* for him; however he did not win the commission to sculpt the huge figure of Neptune incorporated into the fountain in Piazza della Signoria — this the Grand Duke awarded to Ammannati, who responded with the ungainly, awkward giant which the Florentines immediately dubbed *il Biancone* (literally, big white one) a name still used by the inhabitants of the city today. Cellini was furious and he is reported as having said with fiery contempt, 'Ammannato, Ammannato, che bel marmo hai rovinato' (Ammannato, Ammannato, what a beautiful piece of marble you have ruined). Cellini had made the exquisite little figure of *Perseus* for Eleonora of Toledo, finished with gilded highlights on the helmet, hair and boots, now in the Bargello. Later Cellini cast Cosimo I's lifelike portrait in bronze, subsequently adding a splendid armour; the Duke posed for the bust and followed the sculptor's progress almost daily.

There were many artists who worked for the Medici in those years. Ammannati was responsible for the grandiose courtyard of the Palazzo

Pitti and designed the Ponte Santa Trinita after a flood which had devastated Florence in 1547 and brought down the previous bridge. Meanwhile Bronzino was involved in painting the impressive portraits of Eleonora of Toledo, Cosimo, and their children: the delightful fair haired Maria with her face almost like porcelain and the young Giovanni holding a small live bird in his chubby hands. The Grand Duke was patron to these artists and provided that incentive for ambitious projects in order that Florence and the other Tuscan towns could rival the magnificence of other centres, both in Italy and abroad, to the credit and greater glory of the Medici. It was at this time that Giambologna (the Flemish artist Jean de Douai) established himself working for the Medici — a man who had been deeply impressed by the contact he had had in Rome with the elderly Michelangelo and who, having come to Florence on a visit, stayed on in the city for the rest of his life taking his place as principal sculptor at the Medici court.

Cosimo I was, above all, a great politician, keen to strengthen the position of the State so that it might enjoy superiority over the other Italian principalities (it was not for nothing that he managed to secure the title of Grand Duke for himself and his successors among the Lords of Italy). His achievement was in part due to the Spanish support on which he could rely. His wife was the daughter of the Viceroy of Naples who was also Vicar to the Emperor Charles V. He consolidated his power even further when his eldest son Francesco married the sister of the Austrian Emperor Maximilian II. The wedding took place in Florence in December 1565 and was a magnificent occasion. To mark the event, Vasari managed to complete the Vasari Corridor in only five months, and the courtyard of Palazzo Vecchio was completely restored: the columns were refurbished with gilded plasterwork, and the walls were frescoed with views of the most famous cities of the Austrian empire in honour of the bride Joan. The Medici were by this stage related to the great European families and had already given the church two popes.

Cosimo aged prematurely, weakened by the family's hereditary kidney disease, and the grief he had endured at the deaths of his wife and two children within a short time of each other. The death of Giovanni, his favorite child, was an espe-

The Tribune in the Uffizi, created for Francesco I by Bernardo Buontalenti and finished in 1589.

Benvenuto Cellini (1500-1571): Perseus. Loggia dei Lanzi, Piazza della Signoria.

Pontormo (1494-1556):
Deposition.
Capponi Chapel, Santa Felicita.

Rosso Fiorentino (1495-1540):
Angel with lute.
Uffizi Gallery.

cial blow as Cosimo had cherished great hopes for a distinguished ecclesiastical career for the boy. These deaths had been preceded by those of other children: Don Pedricco, Don Antonio and Anna (the title 'Don,' till then unknown in the family, was a Spanish innovation introduced by Eleonora and her Neapolitan retinue). Maria and Lucrezia had died at the ages of 16 and 17 years. Maria, who had inherited her mother's great beauty, had been betrothed to Alfonso d'Este. At her sudden death, her sister became his fiancée in her place. It was this Duke of Ferrara who later became the patron of Tasso (and subsequently husband to Lucrezia Borgia). She married Alfonso, but after three years died of tuberculosis without having given him an heir.

So, out of a total of eleven children, seven died before their father. He was left with only Francesco, Ferdinando, Pietro and Isabella. By 1564 the first Grand Duke had withdrawn from public life,

Vincenzo de Rossi (1525-1587):
Cameo with Cosimo I and his
family.

Bronzino (1503-1572):
Portraits of some of Cosimo's
children.

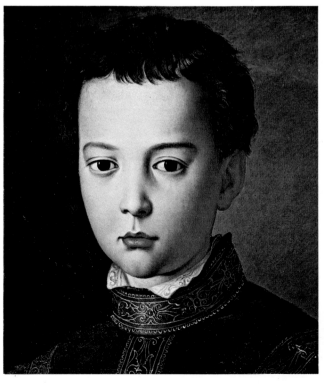

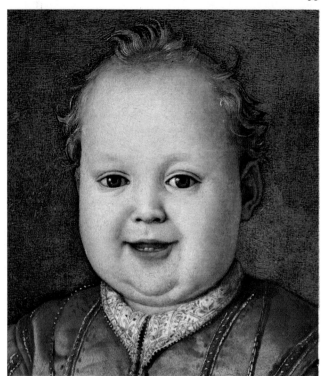

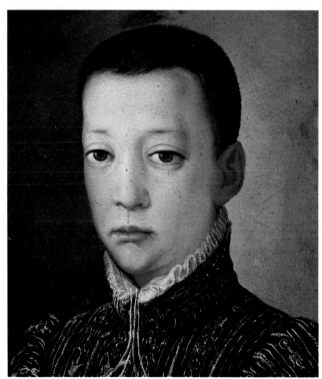

(left) Bia, and Francesco, 1541-1587, the second Grand Duke.

(top row) Lucrezia, 1545-1561, who married Alfonso d'Este and Giovanni, 1547-1562, who died of malaria a few days before his mother.

(lower row) Ferdinando, 1549-1609, third Grand Duke and Pietro, 1554-1604, who killed his wife in the villa at Cafaggiolo.

BELVEDER CON PITTI

officially leaving the reins of government in the hands of his eldest son Francesco (who was given the title of Prince Regent) but nonetheless ready to intervene in the political arena and retaining the title of Grand Duke for the rest of his life. After the loss of Eleonora, he fell in love with a very young Florentine gentlewoman, also called Eleonora, from the Albizi family, and had two children by her: a daughter who died shortly after birth, and Don Giovanni. Indeed he would have married her, had her inconstant and capricious character not dissuaded him; instead she went on to marry Carlo Panciatichi, who had already been banished from Florence for murder and was granted clemency by Cosimo specifically for the occasion. Then the Grand Duke found a new mistress, Camilla Martelli: she too was very young, the cousin of Eleonora degli Albizi, and by her he had a daughter, Virginia, who later (in 1586) married Cesare d'Este, Duke of Modena. The Grand Duke's relationship caused a scandal both in Florence and at the pontifical court. When in 1570 Cosimo went to Rome to receive the much-prized Grand Duke's crown, Pope Pius V put

Justus Utens (?-1609):
Pitti Palace and the Belvedere
Gardens, detail.
Brunelleschi's original plan
for the Pitti Palace before it
was enlarged.

Pietro da Cortona (1596-1669):
Cosimo I presented to Jupiter.
Pitti Palace.
Even after his death Cosimo
was glorified.

pressure on him to formalize his and Camilla's relationship; as a result he married her secretly on 29 March on his return to Florence, although he did not give her the title of Grand Duchess. At the age of forty eight Cosimo, perhaps in part due to the extraordinarily active and eventful life he had led, suffered a cerebral haemorrhage; he partially recovered from this in the loving care of his wife who had by that time become almost exclusively his nurse. But from then on he went into a complete physical and mental decline and finally died at the age of fifty four in 1574.

On becoming Grand Duke, Francesco I (1541-1587), who had never concealed his great antipathy for Camilla Martelli, forced her to leave Palazzo Pitti and retire to a convent, disregarding the role she had played as peacemaker at the most dramatic point in his conflict with his father over his love for Bianca Cappello. Certainly gratitude was not a great Medici virtue.

Francesco had been given a name that was new in the family, stemming from a prayer that Eleonora of Toledo made during a pilgrimage to the monastery of La Verna, that she be blessed with the gift of a son. He was an intelligent young man, particularly attracted to the study of scientific subjects, but not especially given to the art of government despite the extensive tuition he received from his father. The choice of Joan of Austria as a bride for him was greeted with general satisfaction by everybody, including the Emperor Maximilian II, brother of the bride, who thought that he would be able to count on the political

FRANCESCO I

support and, above all, on the wealth of the Medici. Only the engaged couple were not happy with the arrangement. Joan felt that she would be diminishing herself as the daughter and sister of Emperors by marrying a banker (the Medici banks were still active and prospering) and Francesco had by then been hopelessly in love for more than a year with a beautiful Venetian woman who had escaped to Florence in dramatic circumstances. Nevertheless the wedding took place and the extensive celebrations resounded through-

Volterrano (1611-1689): Cosimo and Francesco governing. Pitti Palace. Francesco was named Regent several years before his father's death.

Bernardino Gaffurri (16th century): The offerings of Francesco I. Museo degli Argenti, Pitti Palace

out Europe. It was an unhappy marriage. Joan was rather plain, possibly slightly disfigured, and maintained a disdainful attitude towards all those with whom she had to deal with directly, not for one moment forgetting that she was a Hapsburg and the daughter of an Emperor. Undoubtedly the lack of interest of her husband, who was completely absorbed by Bianca Cappello and by his beloved scientific and pseudoscientific studies, did not help her to settle down and accept either her new family or the court of the Florentine Grand Duchy. From this ill-matched union five daughters were born over a period of twelve years: Eleonora, Romola, Isabella, Anna and Maria. In 1577 the longed for son, Filippo, arrived, but he was to die when only five. Then in 1578, while expecting her seventh child, Joan of Austria died at only thirty one after a fall in the church of Santissima Annunziata.

Francesco was not the only member of his family to make an unhappy marriage, both his brother Pietro — who was lazy and corrupt — and his sister, Isabella — who was called 'bright star of the Medici household' because of her beauty, charm and intelligence — made positively tragic marriages. Isabella had, while still very young, married Paolo Giordano Orsini, Duke of Bracciano. She was as intelligent, refined and brilliant as he was crude, boorish and violent. Isabella, rather like Francesca da Rimini, had found love in the person of her husband's more gentle and cultured cousin Troilo, while Paolo was deceiving his young wife with an unspeakable adventuress, Vittoria Accaramboni, who appears to have put it to him that he should be rid of his wife because she had been unfaithful to him. Paolo Orsini felt that his honour had been outraged. Isabella, realizing the danger of her predicament asked Caterina, Queen of France, for help and protection. But it was too late. Orsini travelled from Rome to Florence where his wife lived for most of the year presiding over an exceptionally

cultured court, and ordered Isabella to follow him to the villa at Cerreto Guidi. There was no escape. The moment they were alone, he strangled her. Then acting in collaboration with his in-laws, whom he had already appraised of Isabella's infidelity, he announced to the foreign courtiers in Florence in a state of agonized grief that his young wife had died 'while she was washing her hair.' Only a few days before, Don Pietro dei Medici had also suffocated his young wife, another Eleonora of Toledo, whom he suspected of being in love with Bernardino Antinori.

Francesco I was an introverted man, gloomy, given to silence, definitely not as good a politician as his father had been; in addition he was distracted by very different interests, particularly scientific and alchemistic studies to which, like so many others at that time, he was drawn because of the element of mystery that they had to offer. He had a laboratory built in the gardens of San Marco and, when he was not at Bianca Cappello's house, used to spend whole days there among gas-

rings and retorts attempting either to melt down rock crystal or to manufacture Chinese porcelain. It was a passion with him to set and make up imitation jewelry and he was the first man to experiment with the working of porcelain and precious stones. Both these commodities were later to prove of considerable importance to Florence: one has only to think of the Doccia porcelain factory and the precious stone works (Opificio delle Pietre Dure) which still exist today. Francesco I was also an intelligent patron of the arts. He was especially fond of Bernardo Buontalenti, Vasari's successor as builder to the Medici, who designed the Tribune for him (the most imaginative and magnificent room in the Uffizi) in the same spirit in which he had fitted out that treasure chest of a study, the *Studiolo*, in Palazzo Vecchio.

Jan van der Straet, called
Stradano (1523-1605):
The alchemist's laboratory.
Studiolo.

The 'Studiolo' (Little Study) of
Francesco I.
Palazzo Vecchio.
Buontalenti designed this
room for Francesco and it
was here that he carried out
his scientific and alchemistic
studies.

Stradano:
The foundry, detail.
Studiolo.

Stradano:
The goldsmith's workshop.
Studiolo.

Francesco was melancholic, the only brightness in his life came from his love for Bianca Cappello. It was not an easy love affair; his family opposed and detested it, and so did the city of Florence. But it was an impassioned love which neither of them concealed and which began before Francesco's marriage to Joan of Austria. The name of the Prince Regent who became the second Grand Duke is always specifically linked with that of the beautiful Venetian. Bianca was born into a wealthy family belonging to the highest nobility (her mother was a Contarini). She fell in love with the young Piero Bonaventuri, Venice representative for the Salviati bank. His background was too modest and his inheritance too meagre to justify his entertaining hopes of Bianca.

The two of them made a daring escape, by sea via Chioggia and Comacchio and then by land across the Appennines to Florence where they were welcomed by Bonaventuri's parents and where the wedding finally took place. The wrath of the Cappello family was unabated however, and they induced first the Venetian Republic, and later Cosimo I to intervene. The Grand Duke summoned them to his palace — this was perhaps the occasion on which Francesco saw Bianca for the first time and fell in love with her.

Soon all Florence was talking about the affair and rumours of it reached the ears of Cosimo and deeply distressed poor Joan of Austria. Bonaventuri undoubtedly gained favours and financial compensation from the situation, as well as the nickname of *Cornidoro* (Golden Horns — a reference to his being cuckolded) from the Florentines. He obtained the fine palace in Via Maggio which was particularly convenient for Francesco, enabling him to get there from Palazzo Pitti in a matter of minutes at any time of the day or night. Bianca definitely reciprocated Francesco's love for her, she may have also wanted to humiliate Joan (who had so far given birth to girls) by providing a male child. But in fact Francesco and Bianca had no children. Nevertheless Bianca had had a daughter by Piero Bonaventuri and looking, as she did, a picture of health she seemed perfectly capable of bearing many children. Bianca sensed that to produce a son would put her above Joan (perhaps the child would one day become Grand Duke), and this child would bind Francesco to her forever. For this reason she faked a pregnancy by bribing three unmarried girls who were expecting babies at the time; whichever gave birth to a son first would be taken on. The girl's name was Lucia, and she was led to believe that her baby had died shortly after birth and that her milk would be used instead for the supposed Medici baby, offspring of a morganatic marriage. Incredibly, Bianca's trick succeeded, at first even deceiving the Court physician whose subsequent silence was probably bought with bribes. Francesco considered himself the happy father of this baby, who was in fact the child of an unknown father. Bianca asked that he should be named Antonio and immediately given the title of 'don.'

Then all at once the truth came out into the open. A girl called Giovanna, one of Bianca's chambermaids, told Lucia — who believed herself to be only the child's wet-nurse and not its mother — exactly what had happened. Then the doctor, who had fallen seriously ill, confessed the story before he died. Meanwhile Joan of Austria had given birth to a prince, the Infant Filippo, who was only to live for a short time. But Francesco's love for Bianca did not diminish. The 'borrowed' child kept the family name and the affection of Francesco who had for some time believed that he was its father. When the boy grew up he became Prior of the Order of the Knights of St Stephen. Then only three months after the death of Joan of Austria, Bianca Cappello secretly married her Duke and he made her Grand Duchess of Tuscany; this was very unpopular with the Florentines who had not forgiven her for her liaison with Francesco and a wicked refrain started going the rounds in Florence: 'Il Granduca di Toscana / ha sposato una puttana / gentildonna veneziana' (The Grand Duke of Tuscany has married a whore, a Venetian lady). The wedding was regarded with displeasure by

Giovanni Bizzelli (1556-1612):
Joan of Austria, wife of Francesco I with her son Don Filippo.
Museo degli Argenti, Pitti Palace.

the family; especially by Francesco's brother, Cardinal Ferdinando who declared (probably with some justification) that his new sister-in-law was an intriguer and even after her death continued to blacken her memory. The secret wedding was then repeated with a proper ceremony in 1578 in San Lorenzo, a magnificent occasion. This event and the title of Grand Duchess reconciled Bianca with her family in Venice who felt hugely flattered by the wedding and sent her some splendid jewelry, in particular a diamond necklace and a grand-ducal tiara. Once her position had been regularized and she had become Grand Duchess, Bianca managed to maintain the dignity of her position although all her hopes of giving Francesco a son were in vain. She was a loyal wife and conducted her life as a princess with decorum and modesty; she was devout and she was charitable. She also tried every possible means (without success) of bringing about a reconciliation between her husband and his brother Ferdinando, despite the fact that she knew he detested her. She certainly had her qualities and earned the award of the Golden Rose from Pope Sixtus V, an honour reserved for queens and sovereigns of outstanding worth and virtue.

But by the time she had reached the age of forty, Bianca's beauty had faded as a result of the

Alessandro Allori (1535-1607): Bianca Cappello, second wife of Francesco I. Uffizi Gallery.
When Bianca died, Ferdinando, brother and successor of Francesco I, had her buried in secret; he also tried to destroy all trace of her. This is one of the few portraits left.

Bronzino (1503-1572): Francesco I.

dropsy which was gradually disfiguring her. Francesco was also in bad health particularly since he had weakened his system with the poisonous chemicals he used in his alchemy experiments as well as by his extraordinary habit of eating either highly spiced or ice-cold food. Their life together was fast approaching its end and in fact they died within eleven hours of each other at their beloved villa at Poggio a Caiano. Here on 8 October 1582 the Grand Duke had just returned from a hunting expedition when he was overcome with shivering and a very high fever; he insisted on looking after himself as he thought best, but there was no improvement. Five days later the Grand Duchess went down with the same fever, and her condition quickly deteriorated. Francesco died after two days in agony. Nobody present had the courage to break the news to the dying Bianca, but she instinctively knew and said to them serenely: 'It is my wish to die together with my

Justus Utens (?-1609):
The Medici villa Ambrogiana
at Montelupo.

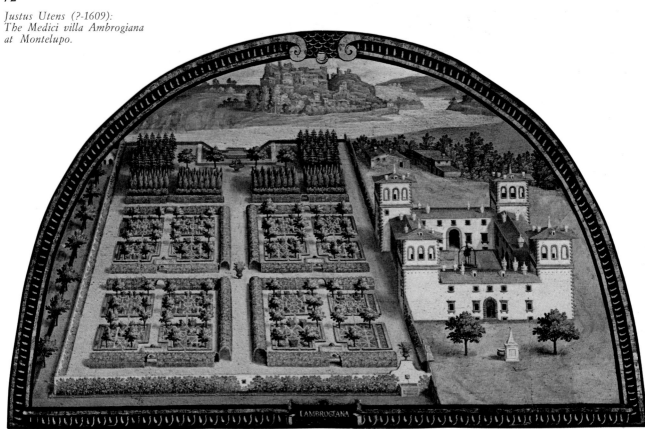

Utens:
The villa of Poggio a Caiano,
detail, where Francesco and
Bianca Cappello died within
hours of each other.

Utens:
The villa at Pratolino, detail,
the favorite villa of Francesco
and Bianca Cappello.

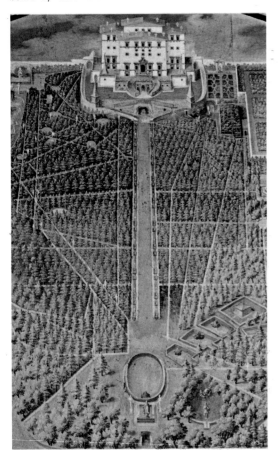

Utens:
*The villa at Castello, detail,
where Cosimo I lived with his
second wife, Camilla Martelli.*

Utens:
*The villa La Magia, detail,
where Alessandro dei Medici
played host to Charles V.*

Utens:
The villa at Lappeggi.

LA PEGGIO

74

*Chapel of the Princes, San Lorenzo.
Constructed by Matteo Nigetti and Don Giovanni dei Medici on a design by Buontalenti. Don Giovanni was the son of Cosimo I and Eleonora degli Albizi. The decoration was done by the Opificio delle Pietre Dure.*

Modern reconstruction of a 15th-century banqueting room.

husband.' She received the sacraments and died.

Afterwards there was talk of poisoned cakes, which the Grand Duchess had personally prepared with the intention of sending them to her enemy Ferdinando, being eaten instead by Francesco by mistake, she joining him immediately after in horror because she knew it would prove fatal. These stories and rumours, spread about most likely to discredit her memory, were given particular credence after they reappeared in popular stories and romantic dramas of the nineteenth century.

The Grand Duke's funeral was, at his brother's request, a grandiose event, full of pomp, with ceremonies held both at the Florence Cathedral and at San Lorenzo. Bianca was buried secretly at night and her grave has been lost without trace ever since. 'Wherever you like, but not with us,' ordered Ferdinando, who subsequently showed himself to be a just and wise prince but who was never able to forgive Bianca's intrusion into the family; 'the terrible Bianca,' was how he always referred to her. Bianca's coats-of-arms and her household goods were destroyed and the villa at Pratolino, which had been Bianca and Francesco's favorite, and which they had made into an idyllic spot decorated with works by Giambologna, was left to decay. It was intended that Bianca Cappello's existence was to be forgotten by everyone; and yet she is perhaps the most vividly memorable woman to belong to the Medici family.

MARIA DEI MEDICI
AND THE THRONE
OF FRANCE

Rubens: Henry sees Maria's portrait.

Rubens: The wedding by proxy.

Rubens: Maria ruling.

When Henry of Navarre became King of France, thanks largely to Medici financing, a marriage was arranged between him and Maria dei Medici. Maria, the youngest daughter of Francesco I and Joan of Austria, was at the time young, fair-haired, very pale and rather attractive to Henry of Navarre, an inveterate womanizer. The marriage contract was signed on 25 August 1600 and the wedding took place by proxy in Florence Cathedral the following December. Among those present was Peter Paul Rubens, as a member of the retinue of his employer Vincenzo Gonzaga, brother-in-law of the bride. Maria was already treated like a sovereign in Florence, with rights of precedence over even her uncles; and feasts, theatrical performances and banquets of unprecedented sumptousness were held in her honour. The galley which brought her from Livorno to Marseille was gilded all over and decorated with French coats-of-arms in diamonds and those of Tuscany in rubies, emeralds and sapphires.

But neither her marriage nor her reign were happy. Maria was not gifted with particular intelligence and unfortunately was too stubborn to heed the advice of her uncle the Grand Duke who tried to teach her how to assume the role of Queen in a country where at court she was looked upon with diffidence if not hostility. In 1608 she complained that her family were treating her like a child, and that as Queen of France she refused to accept what she called 'discipline and control.' Later, she foolishly fell under the influence of two adventurers, her foster-sister Maria Galigai who, with her husband Concino Concini, made a vast amount of money out of her. The final reckoning came later when the Concini were exposed. The husband was stabbed to death and the wife condemned to the stake as a sorceress. It was then that the new minister, the all powerful Cardinal Richelieu, openly took the side of the faction supporting the young Louis and came out against Maria. After a series of almost grotesque incidents, Maria died,

Rubens: Louis XIII comes of age.

in 1642, in the solitude of a convent in Cologne, where she had led a modest existence contrasting strongly with her upbringing as the daughter of the wealthiest banking family in Europe. Her marriage too had been a disaster once the son and heir was born. Henry neglected her to devote himself to a series of amorous adventures, and had little respect for the woman who was his lawful wife.

In 1582 Joan of Austria and Francesco's only son, little Don Filippo, died. And so Ferdinando (1549-1609), who was destined for the cardinalship in the tradition of the great Italian families, became the sole heir of the Medici family. The cardinal who had taken neither his vows nor holy orders though he lived much of the time in Rome in his magnificent villa on the Pincio hill, abandoned his cardinal's hat and became the third Grand Duke of Tuscany. After his father Cosimo, who had created the Duchy of Tuscany as a political entity, Ferdinando was undoubtedly the best of the Medici princes. Intelligent, prudent and well-balanced, he had a strong sense of family dignity and was well versed in the art of good government. With great wisdom, Ferdinando returned the life of the Grand Duchy to a state of tranquility after the general shock of the scandal of Francesco's love for the beautiful Bianca. Ferdinando's qualities were many and wide-ranging. On the political front, he was determined to be rid of Spanish influence and make a new *rapprochement* with France and his distant and powerful cousin Caterina dei Medici. He enlarged and fortified the port of Livorno, opening up what had till then been a fishing port to Jews, Huguenots and refugees from different countries who had been forced to flee their homelands for a variety of reasons — these new inhabitants rapidly transformed Livorno into a city of considerable commercial standing and a flourishing port. He assisted needy students by founding the Ferdinando college in Pisa, and it was at his instigation that the first known convalescent home was opened. He gave further stimulus to the work being done in precious stones at the Florentine factory, by that time one of the projects which meant most to him and which he had done so much to help prosper by chanelling almost its entire production into the completion of the Chapel of the Princes then under way in San Lorenzo. The Chapel was designed by the now elderly Buontalenti and Matteo Nigetti, under the supervision of Don Giovanni dei Medici, son of Cosimo I and Eleonora degli Albizi. Giovanni was another example of an open-minded, intelligent member of the family, a soldier, man of letters and clearly an expert in the field of architecture who was receptive to the new style then just beginning to make itself felt.

Ferdinando was also adept at arranging politically expedient marriages, beginning with his own. He did not want to lose time, and, prompted by his wish to reestablish closer relations with France, obtained from Caterina dei Medici the hand of her favorite niece, Cristina of Lorraine.

FERDINANDO I

Ventura Salimbeni (1567-1613):
The marriage of Ferdinando I
and Cristina of Lorraine.
State archives, Siena.

Anonymous (c 1610):
Tournament in Piazza del
Campo in Siena in honour of
Ferdinando I.
State archives, Siena.

Scipione Pulzone (1550-1598):
Ferdinando I.
Pitti Palace.

Caterina, even after so many years' absence was still nostalgic for Florence. The wedding was arranged in 1587, but postponed first because of the death of Cristina's father, the Duke of Lorraine and then again at the death of Caterina on 5 January 1589, Cristina staying with her to give comfort as she died. Finally in March of that year, the bride left France and travelled to Italy. She was then twenty four years old, Ferdinando was forty. So the original Medici line of Cafaggiolo, of which Caterina had been the last member was joined to the new branch founded by Cosimo I.

It was both a political and a family marriage, but also a good one, blessed by eight children. The private life of the Grand Duke was as straightforward and frugal as his public life was magnificent, and in both he was assisted by his wife's support. Following the political reconciliation with France Ferdinando gave his support to Henry of Navarre, helping to finance his party, thereby winning the latter's friendship and gratitude. Later Henry, by brilliant military and political strategy secured the throne of France, was converted to Catholicism, and was crowned Henry IV. His marriage to Margot, daughter of Caterina dei Medici, had been annulled in view of his plan to wed Maria dei Medici. Henry was conscious that the wealth of the Florentine grand-ducal family was essential to restore the French finances although the French people did not disguise their hostility at the prospect of another 'tradeswoman' on the throne of France. For his part Ferdinando supported the projected marriage and his close involvement helped conclude the negotiations.

Ferdinando I dei Medici died on 7 February 1609 and his reign may be considered as the high point of the age of the Grand Dukes. His rule was that of a wise prince; his reign was peaceful and he showed his concern both for the welfare of his people and for the reputation of the State. With the help of his wife he had developed the life of the court so that it stood as an example of morality, grace and good taste. Cristina of Lorraine, without her husband's guidance, did not show any great political far-sightedness or intelligence. As regent for the eldest of her eight children, the weak and sickly Cosimo, her overriding concern was to consolidate the young Grand Duke's position by leading a near-regal life at court. She made great efforts to increase the power of the religious orders; and so it was that they gradually took over the key positions in the government. In the hands of this new hierarchy the Grand Duchy quickly deteriorated and was soon in desperate straits.

Detail of the decoration of
the Chapel of the Princes.

Medici coat-of-arms in semi-
precious stones.

Piazza della Signoria, in semi-
precious stones .

The first act of the new Grand Duke Cosimo II on his accession in 1590 was a major error in judgment. He closed the Medici banks and would have nothing more to do with any kind of commercial activity, arguing that involvement in business was degrading for a prince, when in fact it was precisely this that had been the principal source of the great family wealth; which, tradition has it, was hidden in a secret room in the Belvedere Fortress. During the reigns of Cosimo I, Francesco and Ferdinando, the bank had continued to flourish providing an inexhaustible source of funds which had been available to emperors and monarchs.

Then there was the equally ill-advised marriage to Maria Maddalena of Austria (unfortunately already arranged by Cosimo's father before his death). Cosimo was eighteen years old, Maria Maddalena twenty one. She was a robust woman, whereas he was slight and ailing. They were not a well match-

Ventura Salimbeni (1567-1613):
Baptism of Cosimo II, son of
Ferdinando I and Cristina of
Lorraine.
State archives, Siena.

Ex-voto with Cosimo II in prayer.

Justus Sustermans (1597-1681): Cosimo II with his wife Maria Maddalena of Austria and his son. Uffizi Gallery.

Anonymous: Tournament in a Medici villa.

ed couple, however eight children were born of this marriage. The Grand Duke was extremely fond his children, deriving inexpressible pleasure from their company and often joining in their games. For the last Christmas of his life, in 1620, he had a kind of Christmas tree put into his bedroom (where he passed most of his time either in bed or sitting in an armchair), possibly the traditional Florentine *ceppo* or Yule log, from which he handed out Christmas presents to the delighted youngsters.

Maria Maddalena was not a woman of high intelligence, but she was gay and full of life: for her, hunting and the quiet atmosphere of gardens meant much more than court ceremonial. She bought the Baroncelli villa on the hill between Porta Romana and Galluzzo, thereafter it was called *Poggio Imperiale* in honour of her royal ancestry; she loved living there and indeed the house became the favorite residence of later grand duchesses too. Maria Maddalena was, however, also a forceful, dictatorial woman, possibly the fact that her husband was always tired and lacked will power reinforced this characteristic in her. He died in 1621 aged only thirty one. There was also conflict in the family between mother-in-

law and daughter-in-law, since they were each determined on a different political course: Cristina would continue to feel the ties of her native France; Maria Maddalena, a Hapsburg, was completely taken up with the idea of a Spanish-imperial alliance. The brief life of Cosimo II was not an easy one with the continual discord between the two grand duchesses; later on their conflict worsened when both of them became regents on behalf of the young Ferdinando. It was detrimental both to the power of the family and to the solidarity of the state of Tuscany, which was already in decline, no longer holding the balance of power as it had in Lorenzo the Magnificent's day, nor the dominant economic and political force created by Cosimo I and Ferdinando.

Owing to his poor health, Cosimo II neglected the government of state, and allowed his wife a free hand in politics, as a result of which Tuscany had to submit to Spanish domination and abandon her ties with France. Nor was Cosimo a patron of the arts. His death was not mourned by the people of Florence who had hardly known, let alone loved him. His sole merit was to have given shelter to Galileo Galilei who was fleeing from persecution by the Inquisition in Padua.

GALILEO AND SCIENCE IN THE GRAND DUCHY OF TUSCANY

During the time that Galileo (1564-1642) was living in Padua from 1592 to 1610, he made frequent visits to Florence where he taught mathematics to Cosimo II. When Cosimo became Grand Duke in 1609, he invited Galileo to come to Florence to live and continue his research there. Cosimo protected the great scientist from persecution and gave him the villa at Pian dei Giullari. This generosity was amply rewarded when Galileo named the four moons of Jupiter that he discovered 'the Medici stars'.

Galileo.

Galileo's magnet.

Tito Lessi: Galileo.

As long as the Grand Duke lived Galileo was safe from persecution: but Cosimo died young, in 1621. His son Ferdinando was still a minor so the regency was in the hands of his mother, Maria Maddalena of Austria and his grandmother, Cristina of Lorraine.

Both women were exceedingly religious, not to say bigotted, and they allowed the Inquisition into Florence for the first time. Galileo had to stand trial before the Holy Office and was condemned to prison. The sentence was commuted to house arrest at Arcetri.

Cardinal Leopoldo, younger brother of Ferdinando, developped the Medicean Experimental Academy, founded by the Grand Duke in 1642 and founded the Accademia del Cimento, *the first European society to devote itself to experiments in natural sciences.*

Ferdinando II at the Accademia del Cimento.

Galileo's compass.

Galileo's astrolabe.

At the time of his father's death, Ferdinando (1610-70), the new Grand Duke, was eleven years old; his grandmother Cristina and his mother Maria Maddalena took on the regency together, in accordance with the wishes of Cosimo II as expressed in his last will and testament. The Grand Duchesses were full of good intentions, but of limited intelligence, in addition, they held radically opposed political beliefs; their main interest was to turn the court into an increasingly ostentatious and luxurious place, and to this end they plundered the Medici coffers which Cosimo II had already depleted considerably and which were no longer replenished by income from the family bank. Both women were very devout, not to say bigotted, and set about increasing the number of religious institutions, monks, nuns and priests until a considerable proportion of the civilian population belonged to religious orders of one kind or another. There were four thousand monks in Florence, quite apart from nuns and priests and it was not long before the greater part of the state systems of education, public administration and even the government itself were under ecclesiastical control, while they themselves enjoyed an excessive and unjustifiable immunity from taxes and personal levies by which the poorest citizens were beginning to be oppressed. Moreover, the Inquisition, which previously had found it impossible to establish itself in Florence, had infiltrated the city and was now imposing its inflexible will from its headquarters in Santa Croce: so the square which had witnessed the jousts and tournaments of Lorenzo the Magnificent and Giuliano became the setting in which the Holy Office of the Inquisition staged its *auto-da-fé.*

Although he had become Grand Duke on coming of age, Ferdinando II was unable to take action against certain instances of religious bigotry until after the death of his grandmother Cristina of Lorraine in 1636 (his mother Maria Maddalena having died earlier in 1617). He was happy to give protection to Galileo Galilei, who was subjected to fresh accusations by the religious tribunals, but sadly, when Galileo died in 1642, Ferdinando II was unable to obtain permission from the religious authorities to give him an honourable burial. Only in 1737 did the last of the Medici succeed in removing the mortal remains of the great man of science to Santa Croce. Perhaps it was for his love for Galileo that Ferdinando II was called 'the wisest of princes and the prince of wise men.' As well as Galileo, he gave protection to Torricelli and Viviani, and founded the Medicean Experimental Academy in

FERDINANDO II

Cameo of Vittoria della Rovere, wife of Ferdinando II. Opificio delle Pietre Dure.

Justus Sustermans (1597-1681): Ferdinando II. Pitti Palace.

Anonymous: Vittoria della Rovere. Pitti Palace.

1642. A major patron of the Experimental Academy was the Grand Duke's brother Cardinal Leopoldo, an intelligent and cultured man who also founded the *Accademia del Cimento* whose motto was 'try and try again.'

The marriage of Ferdinando II was not happy either. Already oppressed by the conflicting influences of his grandmother and mother which accentuated the weakness and indecisiveness in his character, Ferdinando allowed himself to be bound by a long-standing family agreement to marry his cousin Vittoria della Rovere, daughter of Federigo Ubaldo, himself the degenerate and idle son of Francesco Maria della Rovere and Claudia dei Medici (sister of Cosimo II). Vittoria had first come to Florence at the age of one with her widowed mother (the young della Rovere had died in mysterious circumstances) who was, perhaps, happy to be freed from an undesirable marriage which she herself had never wished for.

The two Grand Duchesses immediately saw in the infant Vittoria a future bride for Ferdinando, still a child himself. They called her the little Grand Duchess and prepared her for the role for which she was destined, filling the child's head with ideas of ambition, vanity and a taste for ostentation which was unnecessary given her overbearing pride in her position as the Duchess of Urbino and as the last of the della Rovere line. Her religious devotion turned into bigotry and she combined a taste for unbridled pomp and magnificence together with religious devotion devoid of any genuine sentiment or understanding. She did not share her husband's scientific and artistic interests, but was nonetheless proud of having enriched the art collections of the Medici from her personal fortune. The couple actually lived apart for eighteen years; some said this was because Vittoria found that her husband had certain eccentric tendencies, others that she wanted to punish him for having been unfaithful to her. She was probably a cold and insensitive woman, because during her husband's last illness she only visited him once, and then at his request. She was undoubtedly ambitious, as the vast number of portraits of her demonstrate: in them she is dressed as a goddess, a vestal virgin, or a saint; even as the Virgin Mary with little Cosimo in her arms to take the place of the Infant Jesus. The wedding was solemnised with full pomp and ceremonial on 6 April 1637 and four children were born. Of these, the first two died soon after birth; the third was the future Grand Duke, Cosimo, and the fourth — born after the parents' eighteen years of separation — Francesco Maria,

Justus Sustermans (1597-1681):
Giovanni Carlo, second son of
Cosimo II who became a
cardinal and was also a patron
of the arts and a collector.

his mother's favorite and destined for a cardinalship.

Ferdinando II was a mild man, devoid of ambition. In fact he voluntarily renounced the Duchy of Urbino (which he could have easily demanded after marrying the last of the della Rovere family) in favour of the Papal States. On the other hand he enthusiastically welcomed the art which came to be added to the Medici collections on the death of Francesco Maria della Rovere in 1631. It is quite possible that the political power Ferdinando renounced would have appealed more strongly to the more ambitious Vittoria, who had never ceased to boast of the priceless works of art belonging to her family that she had brought to Florence despite the fact that she had no special inclination towards art herself.

Meanwhile the power of the Medici continued on its inexorable decline, although Vittoria, who was excluded from the running of the affairs of state, cannot be held responsible. However, she was no more successful in the up-bringing of her son, either in preparing him to take on his father's role nor did she try to impress on him the need to improve the quality of life in the state by means of a more open form of politics; instead she preferred to steep him in her own reactionary bigotry.

Ferdinando II had three brothers: Cardinal Giovanni Carlo, a lover of sybaritic life, a patron and art collector who occasionally acted as adviser to his brother; Mattias, a professional soldier; and Leopoldo, who has already been mentioned. Mattias, having been appointed governor of Siena, protected artists and men of letters by founding an Academy of Sciences, Letters and Arts in that city which was similar to and a rival of the Florentine *Accademia del Cimento.* After the death of his grandmother Cristina the Grand Duchy of Ferdinando II saw a last burst of activity during which Ferdinando attempted to weaken the all pervading power of the clergy and diminish the authority of the Inquisition; at the same time following the family tradition, he encouraged the arts and sciences.

However his policies as a ruler had been weak and uncertain, above all dominated by Spain and Austria and extremely oppressive for his subjects whatever their social standing. None of the other Italian states or their inhabitants was as oppressed by taxes as Tuscany or the Tuscan people were. Unbelievably crushing levies were exacted on everything and everybody, and a tenth of all the revenue from this taxation went straight into the coffers of the Grand Duke.

Justus Sustermans (1597-1681):
Prince Mattias, third son of
Cosimo II, later became
governor of Siena.

Giovan Battista Foggini (1652-
1725):
Cardinal Leopoldo dei Medici,
1617-1675, younger brother
of Ferdinando II who founded
the Accademia del Cimento
in 1657.
Uffizi Gallery.

When Ferdinando II died in 1670, his son Cosimo III (1639-1723) became Grand Duke. His long reign, which lasted for fifty three years, was a positive disaster for the state of Tuscany and for the Medici dynasty. Already overly devout in his own right, he had been dominated by the bigotry and vanity of his mother, since his father, whose weakness was indolence, had not asserted his authority in the child's up-bringing. Cosimo spent long hours in prayer and visited monasteries and sanctuaries where he proved a generous and devout guest. Priests, friars and monks proliferated in Florence, absorbed in their psalms and prayers and hymns while the Tuscan state was losing its former brilliance to a steady and reactionary decline for which its ruler was entirely to blame. It is small wonder that Tuscany became the victim of terrible economic recession, as no attention was paid to any of the innovations being put into practice in other Italian states. Even the arts and sciences were neglected in Florence, as artists and scientists left Tuscany which was in the stranglehold of the clergy. Pisa, Siena and Livorno were reduced to insignificant, depressed cities; while Florence's reputation was based exclusively on its illustrious past, which made the present seem even more dreary by comparison. Vittoria della Rovere had taken great pains over her son's upbringing and the end result was a wretched, lazy, weak individual, easy prey for those shrewd malevolent advisers who incited him to persecute Protestants and particularly Jews by creating iniquitous laws whose very existence in Tuscany, which had in the past been such a paragon of intelligent tolerance, seemed impossible to believe. He also made a serious mistake over his choice of a wife: although few young women would have put up with the lethargy and incompetence of Cosimo III, none of them could have been more diametrically opposed to him in character and attitude to life than Marguerite Louise of Orléans. She was the cousin of Louis XIV, the Sun King (whom she may have previously hoped to marry); also she had fallen helplessly in love with another of her cousins, Charles of Lorraine. In fact Cosimo was not unattractive despite being corpulent from childhood, but Marguerite Louise was beautiful: 'of a rare beauty,' remarks Galletti, 'and of an extraordinary vivacity,' as well as being used to the fashionable life at court and French high society. But already in 1658 when Cosimo was nineteen and she was aged thirteen, she had been singled out by the State as the future bride of Cosimo III.

In April 1661 in the Chapel of the Louvre,

COSIMO III

the young princess was married by proxy to the heir to the Grand Duchy of Tuscany, although still in love with Charles and no doubt already feeling a distinct aversion to her new husband. After a few days her ship left Marseille for Livorno where she discovered that the bridegroom had fallen ill with German measles and was not there to meet her. The young couple met for the first time at the Medici villa of Ambrogiana near Empoli. Cosimo was infatuated by the sight of this fair and vivacious beauty; but Marguerite, thinking of her cousin Charles (who had watched her embark at Marseille), and of the French court which she loved, found the reception distasteful and ugly. She was averse to the man who was already, legally, her husband, and particularly repelled by her mother-in-law, who Marguerite sensed was against her and whom she soon wholeheartedly and undisguisedly loathed.

Perhaps Vittoria guessed that the marriage was fundamentally a mistake and would lead to endless pain and misfortune. Perhaps Marguerite intuitively knew that her husband would always be influenced by his mother's bigotry. The bride demanded all the jewels in the crown of Tuscany for herself and when Cosimo refused to give them to her she replied that she would have been better off marrying into the lowliest hovel in France than to ally herself to the Court of Tuscany. This open conflict went on for years, with Marguerite fleeing to villas in the country to be as far away as possible from Palazzo Medici, her husband and her mother-in-law, only ending when the princess returned to France in 1674. Marguerite finally decided that, rather than endure more misery in Florence, she would withdraw from the world in a Montmartre Convent. There had been endless bitter quarrels, escapes on horseback, and she had written furious letters to her husband in which on more than one occasion she had wished that he would go to Hell where she could hope never to meet him again. Three children were born of this marriage: Ferdinando in 1663, Anna Maria Ludovica in 1667 and Gian Gastone in 1671. The births of these children mark periods of comparative tranquility, times when she must have tried to make the marriage work. Then, suddenly, the final crisis broke. Marguerite declared that she had been married to Cosimo against her will and cast doubts on the legal validity of the marriage, going so far as to talk of having been forced into prostitution. There were times

*Justus Sustermans (1597-1681):
Cosimo III, whose long reign,
from 1670 to 1723, was an
unmitigated disaster for
Tuscany.*

when she was out of her mind, but her accusations terrified and confused the intensely religious Cosimo, creating such a crisis of conscience that he felt he was to blame and that his position was against the laws of the church.

Marguerite Louise's departure for France, which she made without the slightest regret at leaving her three young children in Florence, brought some respite to the living hell which had been Cosimo's life.

Of the three young children left behind in Florence, the eldest Ferdinando was a pleasant-looking boy, intelligent and with a natural feeling for beauty and culture, nonetheless he grew into a dissolute and intemperate man. He died before his father, in 1713. Ferdinando was loved by the people, in spite of the fact that his gross extravagance contrasted starkly with the terrible poverty of the great majority of the Florentines. He was, however, a kind hearted man, open by nature and decisively opposed to the hypocrisy of his father

and the court. In his early youth his behaviour was carefree and fun-loving and the people had taken to this; but later his life became vice-ridden and dissolute. He loved music, and as well as inviting Handel to Florence, was the patron of Bartolommeo Cristofori, the inventor of the piano. In his early years in public life he showed real promise and beguiled the Florentines into thinking that, when he became Grand Duke, he would restore Tuscany to its former political and artistic splendour. Quickly tiring of such mild diversions as the court of Florence afforded him he set off on his travels, visiting Venice when one of its famous carnivals was in progress. While there he gave himself over to a life of endless pleasure and immoderate entertainment, becoming involved in a series of love-affairs which led to his contracting an incurable disease from which he suffered for the rest of his life. Meanwhile, in Florence, Cosimo III, after a number of fruitless negotiations, arranged a marriage for his eldest son with Violante of Bavaria, sister-in-law of the French Dauphin. It may have been the case that the depraved Venetian interlude was demanded by Ferdinando of his father in compensation for this unwished for marriage. On his return to Florence he loathed the city more than ever, and despised the life at this father's court which had been practically taken over by friars and prayer-meetings. Nevertheless he bowed to the will of the State and the marriage contract with Violante was signed in Munich on 24 May 1688. After a splendid wedding ceremony by proxy, the princess left for Florence at the end of November. The girl was not yet sixteen years old and there is no doubt that her first meeting with her bridegroom, which took place at San Piero a Sieve, made a profound impression on her. She was at once overwhelmed with love for him. The coronation of the new Grand Duchess took place in the Cathedral of Florence on 9 January 1689. The celebrations to mark the wedding and the coronation were the last great display of Medici ceremonial. Ferdinando was absorbed in his love of the stage, drawing up plans for a new theater in the villa at Pratolino and devoting his attention to Alessandro Scarlatti and music; but his private life was one of waste and dissipation.

Violance, by nature devout, delighted in participating in the religious ceremonial practiced by the Florentine court. But her life was a sad one. She was neglected by her husband who, as a result of the illness he had contracted in Venice, was unable to have children. She never complained openly about this, resigning herself with great dignity to her lot; she became fond of her father-in-law and especially of her brother-in-law, the young prince Gian Gastone, who was generally ignored by everyone: he was a romantic, solitary individual, devoted to his botanical studies and to his art collection. His future was to be no happier than his sister-in-law's. Ferdinando's health had been declining for some years but his wife nursed him loyally without bitterness for the way he had treated her or for the suffering she had had to bear. During this time she prayed, invoking the prayers of others, and she stayed by his side through the successive stages of an appalling illness, which progressed from epilepsy to madness, until his death on 30 October 1713.

After Ferdinando's death, Violante was honoured by Cosimo; in recognition of her outstanding forbearance he gave her a beautiful sapphire necklace and invested her as governor of Siena, a post she held with prudence and wisdom. With the death of Ferdinando, all hope for the continuation of the Medici dynasty came to an end. The marriages which Cosimo III arranged with the specific intention of continuing the family name had failed and left a trail of unhappiness behind. The marriage of his younger brother, Cardinal Francesco Maria, Vittoria della Rovere's favorite son, was no exception. In 1708, when he was already fifty, he was forced to renounce his cardinalship (and, ideed, his carefree life style), in order to be married to the youthful Eleonora of Guastalla, who never overcame her initial revulsion to this elderly, fat husband who suffered badly from catarrh. The wedding was a grotesque farce, held in contempt by the citizens of Florence, as was the moribund Medici court. The marriage lasted only two years, because on 3 February 1710 Francesco Maria died of dropsy 'in the arms of Emanuele the Moor.'

By this time Cosimo III was obsessed by the necessity of continuing the Medici line at whatever human cost, and to this end he arranged a marriage for his second son, Gian Gastone. He has come to be called 'poor Gian Gastone,' because until his marriage became crucial for the survival of the dynasty, he had been neglected both by his grandmother and his father. He was a solitary young man who spent most of his time in a refuge he had in the Boboli Gardens absorbed in his studies of plants and flowers and in his collection of precious objects and beautiful things. He suffered from a deep and inexplicable melancholy. Had his upbringing been more carefully supervised, perhaps he could have become a good prince, not especially intelligent but shrewd and sensible, qualities he had already shown signs of possessing. His rakish uncle, Cardinal Francesco Maria, dragged him into his life of depravity; Cosimo III ordered him to lead an austere and devout life; his sister Anna Maria Ludovica, though loving him in her own way, did not pay much attention to him. He was ignored by his elder brother Ferdinando and by the court and the people of Florence. Only in the person of his sister-in-law Violante did he find friendship and understanding; they were drawn together in adversity. Perhaps he would have preferred to remain unknown and not have had to go through with the terrible marriage his father arranged for him. After the death of his mother, Vittoria della Rovere, Cosimo III came under the influence of his daughter Anna Maria Ludovica, who was most insistent in recommending a German princess as a bride for her recalcitrant brother Gian Gastone: Anna Maria Francesca, widow of the Palatine Count Philip of Neuberg.

Anonymous:
Gian Gastone, youngest child
of Cosimo III and the last
Medici Grand Duke of Tuscany.

Gian Gastone was 23, the same age as Anna Maria Francesca, but descriptions of her appearance suggest that she must have looked considerably older. She was immensely fat, a woman on a vast scale, who left a cultured, sophisticated Florentine like Gian Gastone absolutely cold. On the other hand, she herself was not particularly enamoured at the idea of a second marriage to a young-

er son, feeling herself worthy to be a ruling sovereign. It was the personal intervention of the Emperor which brought this complicated marriage to its conclusion, and the contract was drawn up in Düsseldorf on 4 March 1697. The duchess remained in absolute control of her own property, while Gian Gastone paid the debts and taxes that were owing to the Emperor. The family accepted this unfavourable treatment in the hopes that finally an heir might be born. The couple were to live partly in Bohemia and partly in the *Casino Mediceo* in Piazza San Marco in Florence which had been restored and redecorated especially for the wedding. This took place on 2 July 1697 in the Palatine chapel in Düsseldorf. The marriage was a disaster from the start, based as it was on a lack of understanding, repulsion, and a kind of dejected resignation on the part of Gian Gastone; he was dying of boredom and yearned to be home again, marooned in the house at Reichstadt near Prague where he found no affection or intellectual rapport either with his wife or any of the people in her circle. After an interminable Bohemian winter, he fled to Paris, hoping to revive his spirits. Sent back to Prague by his father, his life was never the same again. He took to drink in order to console and distract himself. Anna Maria Francesca broke her promise and absolutely refused to hear any mention of their going to Florence or to undertake her obligations as a Medici princess. In 1708 Gian Gastone could stand it no longer and returned alone to his native city. Husband and wife never saw each other again. Obviously there was no hope for a Medici heir; all that was left of the family was a wretched prince, a near alcoholic, with a taste for other vices, who spent his days in bed in the grip of a melancholia probably of a psychosomatic nature, unable to react positively or involve himself in anything.

On the death of his father in 1723, he became Grand Duke. He was however no longer able to change either himself or things around him, not least because he was desperately aware of being the last male member of his family; but qualities which had never been recognised previously were revealed in him during the fourteen years that he was Grand Duke. At his wish life at court was conducted in the French manner; he got rid of the most reactionary aspects of his father's bigotry and stopped certain forms of persecution directed against other religions. His court was smaller, less ostentatious and more select in its tastes. For the first few years he still made public appearances, but gradually he reverted to his former life of reclusion, delegating to his sister-in-law, Violante of Bavaria, all official duties and the entertainment of guests (which she carried out until her death in May 1731), and ignoring his sister Anna Maria Ludovica, who had returned to Florence a widow and whom he was unable to forgive for the prominent part she had played in arranging his disastrous marriage. He abolished the death penalty and reduced the price of grain as well as other taxes which had led to suffering

Anonymous:
Gian Gastone dei Medici.
Pitti Palace.

Jan-Frans van Douven (1656-1727):
Anna Maria Ludovica dei Medici with her husband Johann Wilhelm, Elector Palatine. Uffizi Gallery.

and hunger among the populace. He tried to hand on the Grand Duchy to a family who might have been expected to govern it with care without oppressing the citizens of Florence. He was not misguided in accepting the Lorraine family's candidature, thereby showing himself to be an enlightened and openminded prince. When he died on 8 July 1737, he left a deep sense of loss among the people, who had seen little of him but probably nonetheless felt that he was close to them in spirit.

The last survivor of the Medici family was Anna Maria Ludovica, the second child of Cosimo III and Marguerite Louise of Orléans, born four years after Ferdinando and four before Gian Gastone. In 1691 she was married to the Palatine Elector of the Rhine, Johann Wilhelm, a distinguished nobleman with royal connections, the brother of two queens. He was, like his wife, a cultured man; they both knew Latin and Greek, and had some knowledge of modern languages. He was of an open nature, very fond of art, albeit in a more eclectic and superficial way than Anna Maria who had exceptionally good taste like so many of her forebears. The bride was twenty four years old, the bridegroom thirty three. Although their marriage was childless, it was nonetheless perfectly happy, despite the occasional escapades on the husband's part leading to some feelings of jealousy in Anna Maria Ludovica. She, however, was always at his side, and utterly loyal to him even

during the difficult period of the wars of succession. The Palatine court of Düsseldorf was alive to every kind of cultural activity including music, dance and the arts in general. The two sovereigns shared a love of horseriding and hunting. The marriage lasted twenty five years, until the death of the Elector in 1716, a loss which Anna Maria Ludovica bore with great resolve despite her grief. The following year she returned to Florence for good, and met her father at the church of the Santissima Annunziata; he had set aside for her a large apartment in Palazzo Pitti, adjacent to his own, so that he could enjoy his favourite child's company. But there was a clash of personalities between Violante, the widow of Ferdinando, and this proud Electress who felt that she was more a Medici and indeed more of a Grand Duchess than her sister-in-law, the governor of Siena. This conflict did not make life easy for Cosimo who was inclined to take his daughter's side. After the death of the Grand Duke, the situation changed. Gian Gastone, who had never forgiven his sister for her part in arranging his ill-starred marriage and his consequent catastrophically unhappy life, preferred his sister-in-law Violante, the only person to befriend him in the past, and from then on, the two women never appeared together in public.

Anna Maria Ludovica, in the privacy of her own apartment continued to surround herself with precious objects, dedicated herself to religious activity and good works but she was never very popular with the Florentines. She strove hard to have work completed on the Cappella dei Principi (Chapel of the Princes), the great family burial place in the Basilica of San Lorenzo begun by Ferdinando I dei Medici. Her brother, confined to his bed, a voluntary prisoner in his apartment refused to receive her, relenting only as he was dying and even then only after repeated requests from her. Left a solitary figure in the twilight of the dynasty, like a ghost from a magnificent past, she witnessed the arrival of the new young Grand Duke of Lorraine. The Lorraines treated her with honour ad invited her to stay in her family's great palace as long as she lived. There she remained until her death on 18 February 1743. It was carnival time, but as a sign of mourning the Florentines cancelled their usual celebrations.

Anna Maria Ludovica was a woman of many virtues, but the greatest of them was undoubtedly the 'Treaty or Convention of the Family,' a treaty she had personally hoped to see formulated and which she sanctioned in Vienna in 1737 on the death of Gian Gastone. By the terms of this treaty all the art treasures belonging to the Medici family were to become property of the city of Florence and thus, later, form the nucleus of the collections of the Florentine civic museums for the benefit and enjoyment of people from all over the world.

FAMILY TREE

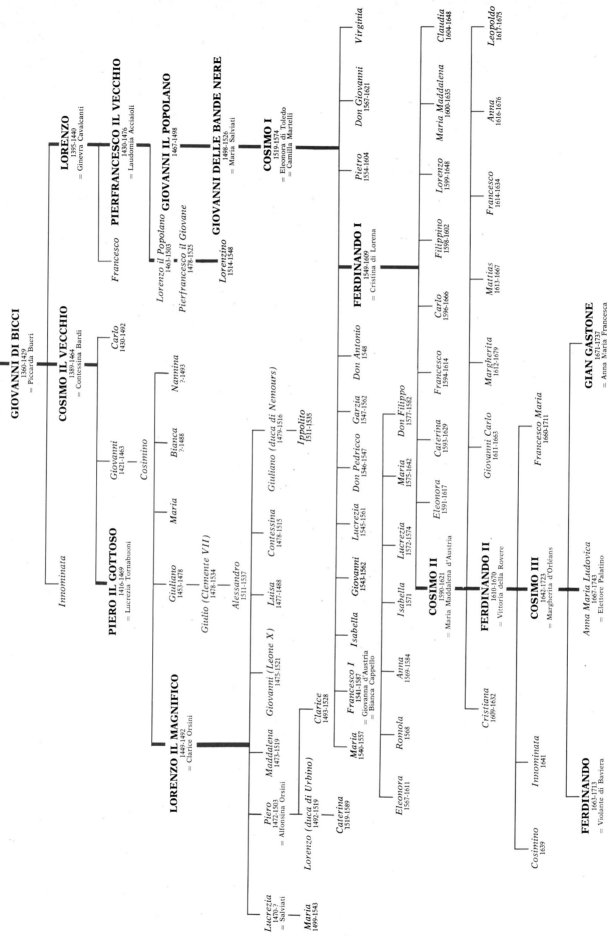